Reflections Through The Window

Ron Sharp

with Michael Clark

Reflections Through The Window

Prison Impact Ministries
Kalispell, Montana

Cover design by Gary Carlson

Table of Contents

Acknowledgements

To my unbelievably brave daughters, Mindy and Sam, who are both caring and loving women that I am so very proud of. They are both continuing to break the cycle of bondage brought about by my own decisions. And to my six grandchildren, who now have incredible opportunities to believe in Jesus.

To my many friends from places all over our great land, those whom God has honored me with, both to know and love, thank you for taking the chance to accept and love one whom the world says is unworthy.

FOREWORD

Who would have thought that Ron Sharp would have written a book about how he came to faith in Christ? In fact, who would have thought that he would even read a book, let alone write one? Better yet, who would have thought that I would be writing an introduction to his book? The answer is no one.

Ron and I grew up in the same neighborhood and became friends at about 11 or 12 years of age. Both of us come from a single parent family. Both of us had alcoholic mothers. Actually, the whole neighborhood was made up of single parent families. So the outlook in life for us wasn't good from the start.

We both belonged to the same gang. We both robbed, stole and pillaged our neighborhood, and a greater part of Des Moines. We both drank at an early age, and did drugs all the way through junior high school. That is where we kind of drifted apart. I was incarcerated at Reform School and Ron was kicked out of school entirely.

That is why it is so amazing that Ron ended up where he is today, a missionary to prisons and a member of Sovereign Grace Church. Amazing grace! That is right – the only way Ron would ever be a member of a church is totally by God's grace.

Ron wasn't a nice guy. He wasn't a pillar of the community. He wasn't a Sunday school boy. Ron was a hoodlum.

This book tells the story of just how this hoodlum became a child of God.

Rev. Michael G. Waters, M. Div.
Sovereign Grace Church
Des Moines, Iowa

Chapter One

A Grim View

I gotta get out of here.

That thought raced through my mind as I poked my head out the second-story window. I had to check out the lawn below where I would make my landing.

As I looked out into the dark, I heard voices shouting from behind me. Then came the sound of feet clomping up the back stairs. They seemed to be chasing me out the window.

"Police! Come out with your hands up!" That was a familiar order for me, but if they were coming in through the back of the house, I could make a quick getaway out that front window.

I stuck one foot out and put my hands on the outside frame, ready to jump. I looked down one more time. Gun barrels stared back at me.

So this was how it would end.

A fiery flash of gunshots, a bloody shootout with no hope for survival, would finish more than a dozen years of drugs, crime, and rebellion. My death would come the pitiful way that so many lives end. At twenty-five, I would leave two daughters and an ex-wife, a mother, three brothers and two sisters, and a thick file at the police department as evidence of my time on Earth.

I had committed dozens of robberies, ingested countless drugs, and cared very little for anyone else. Time in local jails around Des Moines had little impact on me. I had the system figured out and I knew how to work it, I thought.

OK, my only way out is to surprise them. I'll jump out the window and escape.

The only question: Would I hit the ground before I felt the searing heat from a hail of bullets?

I didn't take any time to think about it. I just acted.

It ended quickly.

No guns fired. I just slipped back inside the house and went peaceably that night. An event that was, in a way, out of character with most of the fifteen years leading up to that point.

I see that night in 1973 replayed whenever I look out the back window of my home in Des

Moines, Iowa. The view isn't spectacular. There's nothing that anyone else would call magical, beautiful, or even pretty. But when I stand in my kitchen and look out that window, I can see that little house where my life almost ended. It's just beyond my backyard. I look at the house and I gain a unique perspective on my life and faith. That place was one of a handful of homes in which I grew up forty years ago, but it might be the most important landmark in my past.

My arrest, the last of many in my life, was only one of a long series of events that led me to God. Those troubles kicked off fifteen years before, in 1958, with one tragic death. I trace many problems I faced through childhood and young adulthood to that moment. My father died in February of 1958, when I was just a young boy, ten years old. My father was a carpenter, a house-builder. He and a friend of his, who was an electrician, decided to go into business together. So my father sank every dime he could grab into starting the business. His plan was to open the business in March. He went to work one day in February, had a heart attack, and died. He was 33.

He left my mother with nothing but six children to raise. My older brother was twelve and the younger of my two sisters was six months old. My mother had never worked, as many women didn't in that day. They were housewives and stayed home with their children. With her limited skills, my mother couldn't earn enough money to keep us in the nice quiet suburbs where we lived, so we moved into the part of Des Moines that was considered inner city.

Before my father died, we had a typical American suburban family: Two parents, small children, and most of the comforts that kids crave. I remember times of sledding through winter snow with my brothers and friends in the neighborhood. We all went to the same school, rode bikes together, and played like typical kids. Life was relatively stable. My dad came home from work every day before six o'clock to find supper on the table. We knew he would take us fishing in the summer and hunting in the winter on Saturday mornings. We didn't have many worries; we could have been the typical stable family with the many things that families take for granted until they're gone.

One of the comforting memories of my childhood that I cherish is how my dad took me to work with him in the summer. I was probably eight or nine years old at the time. He gave me a quarter a day to sweep up sawdust and pick up scraps in the homes he built. As I think back on those times, it certainly wasn't the quarter that mattered but the strong feelings of security and love that I felt being around him. Those were obviously lost when he died, with nothing or no one to take their place.

To have that security taken away so suddenly turned our world upside down. The guiding force of my family was gone. We had to move into an area of the city that was so foreign it might as well have been a different country. We were confronted with different rules there, a different hierarchy. The worst trouble awaiting us wouldn't be harmless neighborhood pranks, but drugs, crime, and potential time in jail, where some of my new playmates were undoubtedly headed.

I felt a heaviness in my daily life even a short year later, a hopelessness that seemed to set in almost as soon as my dad died and we had to move. I had just turned eleven years old, an age when small kids should be – and usually are – dreaming about ballgames and other pleasant thoughts. Now, not only was I not thinking about hitting home runs or scoring touchdowns, I was thinking only about survival.

As if I didn't have enough concerns then, I was diagnosed with rheumatic fever. In those days, they didn't know as much about the condition as they do now. The only thing they did know was that in their opinion, the patient needed bed rest. So I was taken out of public school at eleven years old and put in a facility in Des Moines called The Convalescent

Home. The Convalescent Home was mostly for young kids with polio or cerebral palsy – that kind of disability. As far as I knew, there wasn't anything wrong with me. I was full of energy and mischief. They told me I had a bad heart, but I didn't feel like I did. I didn't feel any differently physically. But there I was confined to bed, with young people who had severe disabilities.

Unlike the other kids, who were victims of more severe illnesses, I wasn't bedridden. I would get out of bed and cause more trouble than the staff was ready to handle. I was misbehaving out of hopeless despair and confusion. The staff's way of handling my mischievousness was to lock me in a supply closet, about four-feet-square. If it was around mealtime, I took my meals alone. I welcomed the separation because of my inability to fit into such a place.

I didn't know anything was wrong with me, but I knew my family was disintegrating before my eyes. After my father died, my mother became an alcoholic. She couldn't handle the loss of my dad. And just a couple of months later, her father died. The result of that loss was that she buried herself in the bottom of a beer bottle. All of those things happened around the same time with no one to help me understand what was going on.

I'm not trying to pass the buck. I know that I'm

responsible for my actions.

Being in the convalescent home was my first taste of prison. In this case, though, I truly didn't deserve the one-year sentence. Still, I had no freedom. I had to do what I was told, which was only to stay there and do nothing else. I could look out the window of my room and it seemed that was how I would watch everything happen to my family – through panes of glass.

I suspect that many who read this book would be able to identify with the devastating impact of a tragedy taking place at an early age. Many of us have experienced tragedy, such as the death of a family member, that cripples our ability to grow emotionally. Others of us have lost our entire family. If my saying this has brought something to mind out of your own life and experience, please keep reading. You might just find an answer to your questions about your own life.

I got out of the convalescent home after a year and went back home, where my brother Mike and I began to use drugs. I was thirteen years old when our drug abuse began to take off. We were using drugs, getting involved in criminal activity. It all began when I connected with a small gang of neighborhood kids. We broke into cars, stole things from big stores downtown and sold them. The crime began at a very small level and grew in intensity.

With that recipe for destruction – drugs, crime, and lack of supervision – it was only a matter of time before I found myself in trouble with the law.

My mother was already drinking very heavily. As a result, she met people doing the same thing. She got involved with men who were alcoholics and abusive, both verbally and physically. One recurring childhood memory that brings out an emotional response in me is that she often left us, sometimes for two or three days, forcing us to fend for ourselves. My two sisters were very young. I was about fourteen years old. There wasn't any adult supervision. So as young boys, both my older brother Mike and I were thrust into this situation where we felt like we should be responsible for what was going on around the house. But we weren't capable of handling it.

Many men and women in prison have had similar childhood experiences, maybe abandoned by one or both parents, experiencing all of the feelings and emotions that arise when they're left alone and scared.

One of the ways that I coped with the hopelessness I felt then was to lose myself in the scenes outside the window – both at home and at school. I remember my elementary school teachers writing notes home to my mother. "You know, we really like Ronnie," the notes said. "He seems like a bright kid, but all he does is sit and look out the window. We can't get him to do anything." I don't remember what I was seeing, or if I was seeing anything at all, but I had the feeling that I was alone – not alone by abandonment – but alone by choice, where I couldn't experience the trouble that I knew in my world. If there was a window in the classroom, I could lose myself even in the middle of class with dozens of others all around me. I was escaping.

But there seemed to be little chance of escaping the house, the site of my last capture. We rented the downstairs apartment in that house when I was young. My mother was involved with a guy at the time that was a former prisoner. He'd done time in Iowa, at Fort Madison. He was abusive, tough, physically tough. He came to the house one day looking for my mom. I opened the door. I was still small, weighing about ninety pounds soaking wet. I opened the door. "Yeah, whaddya want?" I said with a cocky tone. "I wanna talk to your mom," he said. "Is she here?" I kept up the cocky tone even more, but I wasn't as tough as I thought I was. "No man, she ain't here," I said as I started to close the door. He threw the door open and took his backhand and smacked me in the face. The force of the blow knocked me across the room, I slid down the wall as he turned and walked out.

That incident was typical of the tough nature of my neighborhood and my life back then. You get hit, you learn to hit back. You live with role models who've been in and out of prison, you think it's a normal way of life. But along the way, you develop feelings of anger and fear that turn to hatred toward the situation you're in and the people you're with. Then, you learn to keep everything but the anger bottled up inside because you can't show fear, you can't show weakness. You just can't.

I now live back in the inner city where I grew up so many years ago. I left not too long after becoming a Christian, after my life began to change. Now, God has me back here to teach me many valuable lessons.

I can now look out my back window and see all that I went through. It's all packaged in that house a block away and all around the neighborhood. As I stand there looking out the window, I don't have far to go to find just a little irony in my life's story. If I turn left to face the window on the side of the house, I can see up the street where my father's house once stood when he grew up here. His house is gone, like him, but it was only a few doors down the street. If I allow myself to think about it, to daydream, I still sense the power of that loss. As a result of what happened in those early years, I missed much of what would have been a normal childhood and young adult life: school, friends, sports, dances, and graduation from high school, and the possibilities of college. I felt the loss throughout those years. I was trapped in a cycle and longed to find a way out.

Chapter Two

Early Lessons

The first time I ever went to jail was in 1961. I was thirteen. My mother let my brother Mike drive her car. Mike was fifteen. The police pulled us over that evening for some traffic violation. At fifteen, Mike didn't have a driver's license, of course. Unlike what police might do today, they didn't call our parents or give us a ticket. In that day, they just took us to jail.

They actually locked us up with adult men in what was then called a "bullpen." Two scrawny little kids in an open room with steel-slatted cots – and a couple dozen men who knew their way around a jail. It probably had room for more than fifty prisoners, but I don't think I would have been more frightened by more men. I was already scared stiff, but because I grew up where I did, I knew that the strong feed on fear. I kept my emotions inside.

I knew that if those men around us saw our fear, they would try to take advantage of us. Rather than allow that fear to surface, I shoved it deeper inside and put on a facade of intimidation.

That same sequence of emotions would hit me later in life, whenever I got in over my head. It became a natural progression: fear, anger, put on a brave front. Hopelessness hadn't yet become part of the sequence.

There were no windows in that bullpen, no views of the outside world to help me escape from that little island. I don't know if a window would have helped because I was too scared to think beyond the danger around us that night. There were men of all sizes and shapes. They shared one obvious marking: They all looked dangerous to two young boys. Any one of them could have slammed us across the cell and into the bars if he wanted. My breaths were short and my eyes didn't rest much that night.

But nothing bad happened. The men — drunks and those who might have been a who's who of the Des Moines criminal world — didn't bother with us. We were released the next morning and something that should have brought shame actually brought a sense of accomplishment. I survived my first night in jail.

With the trip to the bullpen as powerful

inspiration, I learned very early in life that I wouldn't be allowed any emotional outlets. Clam up, live with the pain. That's prison. It's typical and it's devastating to the human soul.

A lack of the grace that comes through the gospel can be even more devastating to the soul. I can blame my family situation and prison for many cruel lessons I learned, but I always come back to the truth that it was my own sinful behavior that had brought me to where I was.

I guess we were Christians in name only – maybe just by identification and the lack of any other faith. We weren't very religious while my father was alive. After he was gone, forget it. We had about as much chance of going to church on Sundays as Iowa had of getting oceanfront property. So I wound up taking the long road to finding faith in my life.

That road took me to the bullpen in Des Moines. That experience made it easier to get mixed up in the drug scene when I was in the seventh grade. I had been to jail and lived to tell about it. If that was the punishment I had to face, I could deal with it. I was part of a group – just eight of us at the most – using drugs, taking alcohol to school, and working our way up the ladder of minor criminal activity. Drugs seemed to be a way of life for us, what people in my neighborhood did. It was almost guaranteed. Plus, I had no adult leadership in my life. My father died and my mother became an alcoholic. She was unable to provide any kind of leadership or any kind of counsel to the family and the only people around us were drug addicts and criminals.

All of the members of that small group of junior high school delinquents were cut off by the rest of the students, to the point that I can't remember getting a date while in junior high – a few girls got involved with us but not many. That's the way it was in school forty years ago. Students weren't involved in drugs, alcohol, or crime. We were shut out by the normal flow of what was going on in school. Now, here we are four decades later, and the situation seems to have reversed. If you're not involved in drugs, alcohol or crime, you're cut off.

So it wasn't a big loss when I quit school at fifteen. I mentally left school when I was in the fifth grade. After that, I was there in body, with my name officially on the rolls, but my mind and interest had left sometime before. I stopped learning at an early age and when I entered prison I was 25 and I had a fifth-grade education level.

On the first day of ninth grade, my friend Jim and I decided we weren't going to school. We had met a couple of girls in downtown Des Moines over the summer. They went to high school in the suburbs and Jim and I decided that we were going to go to their school that day to look up the gals.

Once at the school, we walked in and strolled down the halls, looking totally out of place. This was a high school in the Des Moines suburbs of the early 1960s. Jim and I looked like rejects from the casts of West Side Story or Grease. But we were tough, proud, and on the loose – with our Levi's pulled down to the cracks of our rears.

A teacher stopped us in the hall and asked who we were. We ignored him and just kept walking. He called the principal and together they stopped us in the hall and asked us again who we were and what we were doing there. Then, they told us that we couldn't stay. We weren't surprised, or intimidated. We made some smart-aleck comments and they called the police.

The police came to school and arrested us. They called our junior high school and told the principal that they had two of his students in jail. The junior high principal wasn't pleased. "Well," he told them, "just keep 'em because they aren't coming back here again." That was the end of school for me. They wouldn't allow me to go back to school there – or anywhere else. But that was fine with me. I left and never looked back. You can say it was a mutual decision.

It was a turning point for me, too. I realized that the traditional way of looking to the future was over. School was over. My options were slim to none.

Life without school spared me the annoying pressure of putting up with teachers I didn't respect and sharing my time with students who didn't like me. Just for the record, I couldn't find much to like about them, either. But life for a junior high school dropout was also very limited. I bounced around without anything significant to latch onto – save for the drinking, minor drugs, and petty crime.

One of the foolish criminal activities that I wasted time on during those years shows how the criminal mind works: some innovation but short on ambition. During those formative years, when we were just beginning to build a respectable criminal record, my friends and I had a key to the parking meters in Des Moines. One key fit them all back then – if it doesn't still. One of our fund-raising activities each day was to take money out of these meters, but not all of it.

We had to show some discipline because taking all the money would alert the police – or at least the meter maids. They would catch on that somebody was getting into the meters and grabbing the change. But if we took just a little money out of each one every day, they never knew. So every day, we took our share of the city's parking proceeds out of the meters.

As those early teen years went by, I couldn't help but think that I had to find something better. We worked to steal little things like parking meter change or other petty thefts with the goal of buying enough drugs to get high. We didn't go after any big scores, no armored car robberies, no big bank heists. We just lived for the short-term goal of getting enough drugs to make ourselves feel better soon. That was the way I lived back then, but I don't think I really wanted to become a career criminal. There had to be something better out there.

In 1965, my cousin Ricky and I hatched a plan to join President Johnson's Job Corps. The first center had just opened in Texas, on a piece of land donated by Johnson himself. They were recruiting young boys to go there to learn vocations. So Ricky and I signed up for the program. I remember the feeling of excitement, the plans we made and the possibility of getting out of the mess we knew we were in: the inner city, the crime, the drugs. We saw the Job Corps as an opportunity to change our lives and start on a new road.

Well, Ricky would get a chance to take that road. They accepted him and rejected me because of the heart condition left by the rheumatic fever.

The disease scarred a couple of heart valves – I still have trouble with them to this day.

Ricky joined the Job Corps and wound up in the program that gave him a half-day of heavy equipment operation and mechanics and a half-day of regular army boot camp. When he was 17, he went into the army, which probably would have happened to me.

He got married and the relationship he had with his wife must have helped him become stable because he didn't continue the cycle or go through all of the troubles that I did. He had a purpose. It was the Job Corps and the Army that got him out of the mess that continued to surround me – or the mess I continued to surround myself with.

After all these years, I don't know what rank he attained, but I know it's been his career. Starting back in '65, and even to this day, I can't stop myself from wondering what if.

Denied a chance at a future, I hardened a little. Instead of things getting better, they got worse. They intensified. Within months, I began to move deeper into the drug world as a criminal bent on supporting the habit and lifestyle of an addict.

When people mention the '60s, they talk about the "free-living" mentality of the times. Peace, love, and anti-establishment thinking. But for me, and anyone else who grew up in the inner city during those years, it was something different altogether. We weren't rich kids from the suburbs who all of a sudden chucked it all to experience freedom, smoke a little marijuana, try LSD, and take a van to California. All of that was happening, but for those of us in the inner cities, the drug culture was a way of life. (It always had been, it might always be.) It didn't feel like something we made a conscious choice about. Our friends were doing drugs and most of our role models were getting high, too. Or at the very least, they weren't around to make sure we weren't.

Drugs were our way of life, a condition of our existence. We weren't taking them to make any statement. They were our primary form of entertainment and a way of proving our independence. I would have loved to be part of Woodstock. I often say that I would have been at Woodstock – if I hadn't been in jail. That's true. Some friends and I were planning to go, but I was arrested and put in jail – and they never gave me time off so I could attend.

I didn't need a trip to Woodstock or a window to help me mentally escape jail that time. I would have liked to see a vision of my future, though. If I could have known what was ahead for me, I might have avoided it.

Chapter Three

The Wages of Crime

I never graduated from high school. I got a GED in prison, but there was no cap, no gown and no walk across the stage. About the time I would have finished high school, though, I did graduate to big time crime. No more ripping off parking meter change for me. For about three years, beginning when I was seventeen, I was part of a burglary ring in Des Moines.

I had two partners. Nick, who was a few years older than me, and another kid named Joe, who was a couple of years younger and grew up in a small farming town near Des Moines.

We were an interesting team of thieves. They could always find me, the drug addict, somewhere within the known boundaries of the Des Moines drug world. Nick was a family man, so we could always find him at home with his wife and three small kids. He didn't drink, didn't use drugs, and didn't run around. Stealing was his job and he was extremely good at it. Joe was a really handsome, blonde-haired guy who happened to love prostitutes. There was a known prostitution area in Des Moines, so we could always find him there, laying up with some prostitute. We were three guys with totally different backgrounds and interests. The only thing we had in common was that we were thieves. Outside of burglary, stealing, and fencing what we'd stolen, we would never have gotten together. It wasn't like we were buddies, but professional colleagues.

We were the actual gang who broke into houses and business and ripped people off, but we also had contract help. Yes, even criminals know the business value of hiring part-time or temporary help. For the three of us in the gang, and the two guys we hired on a contract basis, crime was a job.

Our hired contractors gave us leads and helped pick out the best marks. One guy drove a taxicab. He didn't drive the cab for a job so much as he did it to find the best prospects for us to rob. He was incredibly good at it, too. He could pick up a fare at a downtown bar or nightclub and pump them for information in the few short minutes that he had them in his cab. These people usually had gotten off work and gone to bars with friends. When they had too much to drink, they didn't want to drive home and called a cab. If our guy knew he was driving the person to a nice neighborhood like Waterbury Circle – a very wealthy part of Des Moines – he'd use the twenty-minute ride to get all kinds of information from the passenger.

He'd ask them if they had a vacation planned, when it was, how long they'd be gone. He'd find out if they had a dog, a burglar alarm, or if they had expensive paintings or coin collections; anything of value that we could get rid of easily. You know how gabby some people can be after a few drinks. They usually told our cab-driving friend anything and everything. For him, it was just a matter of getting the right information, and this guy was good at it. Then he'd sell the information to us. "These people live at this address," he'd report. "They're going to be on vacation next month, these are the kind of things they have in the home. Yes, they have a dog. No, they don't have a burglar alarm."

Armed with all of the important information we would need, we went off and did the job.

Like any good businesspeople, we made sure we had information from more than one source. We had another fellow work for us on a contract basis. He would dress up in a suit and tie, looking like the average successful businessman, lawyer, or high-ranking insurance executive downtown. He'd go into a bar or nightclub and find his way into a conversation already going on between two or three other guys. He would just pull right into the conversation and, before long, be part of the group. Within a half-hour or so, he'd get the same type of information: address, vacation, valuables, and pets and alarms. Then, he sold the information to us.

That was the "acquisition" side of our business. For "distribution," or turning what we acquired into profits, we had a fence, a guy who owned bars and other establishments all around the state. He bought our stuff and then turned around and sold it for his own profit. We stole three nights a week and then spent one day fencing what we'd stolen. Unlike other businesses, we gave ourselves three days off each week.

Throughout our careers as burglars, we never felt any regret. There was a lack of consciousness about it, no feelings of remorse. We weren't physically hurting anyone. It was all just business and so simple that we never bothered to think that the whole operation just wasn't right. Although, I don't think that we would have stopped if we had thought about it.

Not all of our jobs went according to our business plan, though. Every enterprise suffers setbacks, but I doubt many businessmen can they endured what we went through one night in 1966. Our fence told us about a cigarette warehouse in Des Moines. He knew about it because the distributor who owned the warehouse stocked the cigarette machines for his bars in the city.

One night, Nick and I decided to break into the warehouse. Joe wasn't with us that night, but we didn't think we needed him for the job.

The biggest problem was that the building was right down the alley from the police station. Standing on the street and looking into the alley, we could see the police going in and out of their precinct building. But we had cased the warehouse for a while and saw that it didn't have a night officer, a security guard known as a "hack." And we knew it had a burglar alarm on the lower-floor windows.

Risky or not, we decided to go ahead and break into the warehouse. We stole a U-Haul truck and backed it up to the loading dock. We knew we had to avoid the lower windows and the alarm so we went up the fire escape, which was the only way to the roof. We knew the roof of the three-story building did not have an alarm. Once we got up there, we tore a hole in the roof.

So far, everything had gone according to plan. We threw a rope in the hole and got ready to slide down into the warehouse. But before we went in, we decided to sit down to have a cigarette. It seemed to be a good way to rest for a moment and celebrate our early success. Then, while we were puffing on our cigarettes, a light shot up out of the hole. As the light beamed through the hole, we could hear police climbing up the fire escape. We were trapped.

Nick and I had no way out. We had to jump off the building. It was three stories off the ground, but we hung from the ledge and jumped. When I hit, I sprained my ankle. Even worse, we had jumped into a courtyard between the cigarette warehouse and the building next to it – four walls surrounded us and we had no way out. Trapped again. We looked around and spotted a hole that led into the building next door. We jammed ourselves through that hole and then went under the wood-planked floor of the building. We could hear the police walking around on the floor above us, shining their lights and talking about the possibility of us being somewhere in the building.

We weren't in our little hole beneath the floor too long before I heard some squeaking noises. I asked Nick if he could hear them. "Noise?" he asked. "It's nothing, just the floor settling." Then I felt something run across my leg. I was afraid I knew what it was. The squeaks, the feeling of the light tapping across my leg. I just didn't want to know for sure that I was right. We lay there in the hole for three hours.

After we were sure the cops had left, we crawled out from our hole, out from under the floor. As we walked a couple of feet across the floor, Nick picked up a loose floorboard. A dozen rats in a nest scattered in all directions, squeaking out their own alarm! Now I knew what had run across my leg and made those squeaking noises around my head. The thought of lying in that rat's nest still makes the hairs stand up on the back of my neck.

We left the building but we weren't out of trouble yet. Once we were out, we still had to go through the courtyard again to get back to the street. We stayed away from the cigarette warehouse because we knew the first-floor windows had alarms. That meant that we had to break into the building with the rats that we were just under and then break out of it again.

We were barely out of trouble, we thought, when we got back on the road. We began to walk back to the car several blocks away, where we'd left it, but we were filthy dirty and my sprained ankle made it very hard to walk. Then, we heard someone shout. "Halt! Put your hands in the air!" he said. "Turn around."

It was the police, and maybe the same ones

who had walked the floor above us while we were lying in the hole. They started pumping us with questions. "Where were you tonight? What have you been doing? How did you get so dirty? What happened to your ankle?" We told them we were walking from home and crossing the railroad tracks on our way to a bar nearby. Thinking fast on our feet, we told them that I slipped on the tracks and that I slid down a slope and had hurt my ankle and that Nick had gotten dirty by coming down to help me. Somehow they bought our story. Or, maybe they just figured that they didn't have near enough proof to charge us with breaking into the cigarette warehouse.

We had escaped again! Except when we got back to the spot we'd left the car, it was gone. The police had towed it after finding it in the parking lot where we had left it. We figured that they had taken it to the impound garage. The only thing left to do was to break into the impound garage building to get our billfolds out of the car. We had left them there so we wouldn't accidentally lose them while doing the job. If they bothered to search the inside of the car, they'd find the billfolds and figure out that it was our car they towed from near the warehouse. That might be enough evidence for them to at least arrest us, if not make the charges stick.

So we had to break into the garage to get our wallets out. But that was a rough night on the job. It was another moment that made me wonder if I couldn't find a way out of the life I was leading. There had to be a better way. I even brought it up to my friend Nick on the way home. "I think I'm going to get a job," I told him.

But I didn't. And it would be several more years before I moved closer to the belief that I could get out of the cycle of drugs, crime, and hopelessness. Maybe there was a reason for that, a reason I couldn't know or understand yet.

In so many ways, my story could have been written in the Old Testament.

2 Kings 17

13 The LORD warned Israel and Judah through all his prophets and seers:

"Turn from your evil ways. Observe my commands and decrees, in accordance with the entire Law that I commanded your fathers to obey and that I delivered to you through my servants the prophets."

14 But they would not listen and were as stiff-necked as their fathers, who did not trust in the LORD their God.

15 They rejected his decrees and the covenant he had made with their fathers

and the warnings he had given them. They followed worthless idols and themselves became worthless. They imitated the nations around them although the LORD had ordered them, "Do not do as they do," and they did the things the LORD had forbidden them to do.

Many times I was told by others that I was on my way to somewhere I didn't want to go. But some people just need more lessons than others and I wasn't near the point yet where I would realize that I had to change inside.

Chapter Four

God Has A Plan

All right, I'm goin' out the window, I thought. Freedom was just one floor down.

Police were closing in on the bedroom in that Des Moines house the night I was arrested in 1973. I might not have known where I wanted to go with my life at that point, but I knew I didn't want to go to jail. The way out was through that window. Sounds simple, but there was quite a journey in store for me.

Up to that point in my life, I thought it was practical just to take the shortest route for everything – I didn't know any other way. If somebody else had something I wanted, I just took it. That really was all of the motivation I needed to rob someone or break into a building and steal something. I had become powerless over my own actions and I did it lots of times.

I had been a part of so many robberies and crimes in my young life – at least dozens into my mid-twenties.

One night, a couple of years before my last arrest, my brother, me and another fellow broke into a drugstore and took all of the drugs – or at least all we could find and carry. There was so much irony in that crime. I don't really know what we'd planned to do with all of them; use them, I guess. We had what looked like a few months' supply of barbiturates, diet pills, morpheme, and others. We could eat them and make the supply last awhile, but not very long – maybe a few weeks because we weren't drug pushers. I didn't sell drugs professionally. When I had drugs, I might sell some of them in order to obtain something I wanted. In that sense, I sold drugs.

But the whole scene of selling drugs as a criminal business was always a bit "out there" for me because you know that anything can go wrong at any given time. It's not like breaking into a building and having some control over the outcome. The only thing that could go wrong is that you get caught. There was some risk of getting shot, but not as much as with drugs. If you sold drugs, you could get killed, robbed, or maybe get caught dealing to the narcs. Of course, there was always the danger that the people you were dealing with were somewhat less than honest. I always felt that there was enough unknown about it that I didn't like being a part of it, so I never got involved.

But stealing drugs for my own use, that seemed to be OK with me. In my twisted way of looking at things, I knew only what the streets had taught me. Another night, after a different drugstore burglary, my brother and another friend and I were busy celebrating our success. We had just scored a carload of drugs and made it back home, where we sat down on the floor to divide the drugs we had stolen. We probably had three or four suitcases filled with the stuff. The three of us took the bottles and tossed them into a heap on the floor. We were separating them by type, bottle by bottle, when we got into an argument. The argument quickly turned into a fistfight. Imagine three guys loaded on drugs in a small living room with a mountain of bottles, pills flying everywhere, wrestling and punching each other in a knockdown, drag-out fight. It sounds pretty stupid, doesn't it?

I couldn't see it then, but that fight scene was a perfect example of the futility of crime. We had just stolen from the drugstore, we had plenty of drugs to give ourselves the short-term pleasure we craved, and we still didn't have all that we wanted. We were willing to fight each other because we weren't sure we were getting our fair shares of what we'd stolen – what we'd gotten for free. How bizarre is that?

That should have been a sign that would keep us from stealing again, but I guess we weren't looking for signs. Did we think we would go on robbing and burglarizing until we were old and gray? No, but we never thought about the future beyond the next day or two, either. We were trapped and it was the simplest way to get through life. As simple as jumping out a window and dropping one floor down.

The last crime I committed, the one that brought me to that window, was an armed robbery. We busted into a Des Moines drugstore and held it up for all the drugs we could carry. We might have been bold, just not very sophisticated – and when you're loaded, how sophisticated can you be?

There were two high school-age girls working inside with the elderly man who was the pharmacist and owner. We tied him up. At one point, one of the girls asked me if we wanted the money. We weren't there for money, but why refuse? "Yeah, why don't you put it in a paper bag," I said when she asked. Then, we poured bottles of pills off the shelves into boxes. We went to the areas that we knew held the kinds of drugs we were looking for: Speed, barbiturates, morpheme, demoral, and so on. We put them in boxes and took them out the back door, leaving the three people inside. But as we left the drugstore, someone driving by spotted my license plate and called the police. The license plate led them to the house where we were once again dividing drugs between us when they came for us just two hours later.

When the police got there, they closed in. They were on the way up the back staircase when I heard them and began to go out the front window. "This is the police!" they said. "Open the door, we have the house surrounded."

The police had the house surrounded that night, but drugs had surrounded my life for more than a decade before the arrest. I couldn't seem to do anything for too long if drugs weren't stuck in the situation somehow. Sometimes the results were bizarre, sometimes they were nearly disastrous.

A couple of weeks before the drugstore robbery, I went on a drug spree, shooting speed for three or four days. I hadn't slept, I hadn't eaten. I decided that I needed to get some sleep, crash awhile. I started shooting barbiturates, mainlining sleeping pills. But they didn't knock me out. When I left home one night, it took me four hours to walk four houses over. How? You become so paranoid after being up that long and taking the kinds of drugs that I was taking that you see shadows and things that aren't really there. For four hours, I was ducking behind bushes, thinking I was seeing police or something threatening. It took daybreak to show me there wasn't anything there after all. It was a night of darting and ducking, hiding for what seemed like a couple of minutes but was really hours. I made my way to my mother's home where I shot barbiturates until I passed out. When my mother found me, I had blood coming out of my mouth, ears and the corners of my eyes – obviously half-dead and maybe I should have been. I was awakened by her scream. I got up, took a bath, and began to shoot more drugs.

One near disaster came when I overdosed on heroin. My brother Mike walked me around the neighborhood for two or three hours, keeping me awake. One of the dangers of heroin is that if you OD on it and fall asleep, you're likely to stay asleep for good. You have a better chance to survive if you can stay awake. So when my brother walked me around the neighborhood, holding me up most of the time and keeping me awake, he probably saved my life.

Not that I cherished life that much back then. I was alive one day with no guarantee to stay that way until the next. I wasn't suicidal, but I did my best, it seems, to lessen the odds of survival. God must have wanted me alive, for His own reasons that were unknown to me. Otherwise, there were many nights that I could have died. Once, while in a bar in Des Moines, my brother, a friend and I got into an argument with a couple of guys. It quickly turned into a gun battle once we took it outside. It was a miracle that no one was wounded or killed that night or else I still would be in prison wondering when I might get out.

My life in those years was much like that of many prisoners, those behind high walls and fences as well as those lost and trapped in bondage to their own rebellion. I had no idea of all the things that God had in store for me in the future. He had a plan even if I didn't have any idea what it was. It makes me think of these verses that have become so powerful in my life:

Jeremiah 29

11 For I know the plans I have for you," declares the LORD, "plans to prosper you and not to harm you, plans to give you hope and a future.

12 Then you will call upon me and come and pray to me, and I will listen to you.

These plans lead to salvation for those who are His sheep.

John 10:27-28
My sheep listen to my voice; I know them,
and they follow me. I give them eternal
life, and they shall never perish; no one
can snatch them out of my hand.

I could have spared myself so much pain and
trouble but I am who I am in Christ as a result
of it. I remember after I was convicted of that
last drugstore robbery, I went to Anamosa State
Penitentiary and was standing in the rotunda area,
five feet wide by seven feet long. Out of one side,
I could see beyond the door I entered, the hall that
led to freedom. When I looked the other way, I
could look directly down the hall into prison,
where I knew I would spend my time and face the
unknown for the next few years.

As I stand in front of my window looking out
at the house where I was arrested, I sense and feel
the loss. But I also have incredible thankfulness for
how God has kept me as I went through all of it. He
has brought me to where I am today.

Getting to my present age of 53, being alive
and enjoying the life I now lead, would have been
impossible if I'd continued on the criminal path I
had taken to prison in 1973, at age twenty-five. I
didn't really know how to function according to
the rules of conventional society. I only knew how

to live by the code of the street. Get a real job? I never saw myself climbing the corporate ladder or becoming a hotshot executive. I also didn't see too many job prospects for a kid with a résumé that highlighted an active criminal career – and a disregard for the morals behind the laws he broke.

So, despite having an idea before I went to prison that I wanted to change, it would have taken something close to a miracle for me to get a job – and hold it for long – at that point in my life. So I just stayed on the criminal side of the fence living within the trap I had created for myself. It seemed to be easier for me, and it's all I really knew.

I did have some very brief spells when I had chances to change and even found work. They were just short-lived.

While I was doing a stint in the county jail for breaking and entering in 1969, the judge agreed to let me out on work release. I just had to find a job. Well, how do you find a job when you're in jail? It's not the sort of return address that makes employers jump to hire you. But I went through the want ads anyway and wrote some letters. One of the letters I wrote was to a casket company in Des Moines. They sent a guy over to interview me at the jail. I wasn't wild about building caskets, but I'd grown up around carpentry and had some knowledge of it. It was a good job and I had a chance to get it.

Plus, I didn't have a list of job prospects to pick and choose from.

But the casket guy hired me. During the day, I left jail to go to work, which was about seven blocks away. I didn't have long to get there. They timed it out for me. "You've got twenty minutes to get to work in the morning," I was told. So twenty minutes from the time I left the jail, they might call the company to see if I'd arrived.

I had the same amount of time to get home, but I also had a friend who was an officer in the jail. For a carton of cigarettes, I could buy an extra fifteen or twenty minutes of freedom. With that time, I met up with Mary, my girlfriend at the time.

The next thing I knew, Mary was pregnant and I was getting married in jail. I was twenty-one, she was sixteen.

I thought it was the right thing to do at the time, but I can see now that it wasn't a very bright thing to do. Drugs and prison helped finish my relationship with Mary – we had two daughters and saw our marriage last for only a few years. Mary and I had separated before the last robbery and out of three years of marriage, I probably lived at home for maybe a year.

I wasn't a fit husband or father. Drugs guided me, and Mary as well, on a selfish path. Get high, come down, get high again. Commit robbery or some other crime to buy drugs to get high.

However, I do have two wonderful daughters and their children that came from that not-so-smart decision, and what a gift from God they are. It definitely wasn't a formula for success or a romance story you'd find in a bridal magazine.

I didn't make a lot of smart decisions in my youth. I'm reminded of my failings – and the good things that I have now that I didn't deserve in those days. Outside of Christ, I still don't deserve them. But whenever I see the house a block away and think about what might have happened if I'd jumped out that window, I can't help but feel fortunate. Better things were ahead for me because of a choice I made, but not before I had a lot of work – and learning – to do.

Chapter Five

Lessons Learned Through the Window

As a schoolboy looking out the windows of all of those classrooms, I just stared at whatever scenes lay beyond the glass. I didn't try to focus on specific people or features of the landscape, I just felt the pull to be out there, somewhere other than the classroom where I was so uncomfortable.

I wound up experiencing many of those same feelings again in prison, where inmates know the physical limits of being in a cage, able only to look out. But, like my school window gazing proved, prisons can be made of more than just physical surroundings. I look back now and see that a few years after my conversion, I still had areas in my life that caused me to fall back into feelings of hopelessness. Those feelings would generate memories and frustrations of the incarceration period and the life of a prisoner.

I often discuss my feelings with prisoners because many of us can get a good grasp on how much God loves us, but for those of us who have been separated from mainstream society and can't relate to being a part of it, we always see ourselves in a cage looking out.

Boyhood window gazing offered an escape from the years of devastating things that happened to my family. Later windows – with bars on them – offered other views, scenes that weren't filled with the lifestyle of drugs and crime. But on the inside of the window, my side, I still felt trapped. I didn't know how to grasp all of the things that I felt at the time. I just wanted to be on the other side.

But the other side is far from ideal. There is even a separation between the real world and the faith world. I learned that as I became more faithful to God after I got out of prison. I still thought of myself in Earthly ways and, because of that way of thinking, I couldn't understand how God's love worked in my life. I make a point of telling prisoners that they may never feel complete when they get out, that there is no "end zone" where life is perfect. But one of the ways that we, as Christians, overcome the feelings that we sometimes have is to keep our thoughts on the end of the road – the goal, as God calls it.

It's extremely important for prisoners to

understand that society may never forgive them.

There's probably a better chance that it won't forgive them. Unless they come to grips with that possibility, they won't face their troubles. They'll do what I did, what most inmates do, they'll try to hide.

It's like what Adam and Eve did after they sinned. Where did God find them when He came into the garden? Hiding. What do we do when we sin? What do we do when we feel like failures, like everyone's against us, including God? We still run and hide. Not behind trees, but within ourselves. We isolate and we shove all of the feelings and pain down deep, or we try to numb them, simply because we don't want to face them. That's what Adam and Eve tried to do. They didn't want to face the truth, but God called them out. He made sure they faced not only Him, but themselves.

That's one reason why so many prisoners, if not most, spend so much time "numbing" themselves with drugs. If you've never had the pleasure of a penitentiary tour, a prison cell doesn't offer much of a view. Inmates can make their own drug-induced window to get away. It's easier and more comfortable to get high and block the pain than to face the reality of our crimes and how they might have impacted us and others.

I numbed myself often, but the process didn't

start in prison. I was moving through the cycle of hopelessness before I got to prison, I just brought it with me. Throughout my teenage years and into my twenties, I was arrested many, many times. I would be arrested and charged with several different felonies, but one of the court's tactics to get a conviction and send someone to prison was to keep them in jail, isolated, long enough that they would confess just to get to prison, just to get out of their little jail cell.

It's a strategy that doesn't make any sense, but it works. Someplace else, wherever it might be, is better than a small cell in a local jail. In prison, you have more room; you have more things to do. In a jail cell, you think, "Here I am just sitting here. All I know today is that I want out of here. If that means I have to go to prison, that's fine."

Where most guys would say, "I can't stand this, I can't take this anymore," I didn't mind sitting in jail. It didn't affect me the way it did a lot of people. I was a master at finding my own windows to look out of. Therefore, I would never confess. I would say things like, "You know what? You can keep me here as long as you want to, but I'm never going to plead guilty to this. I want you to understand that right now. You can keep me here a year. It doesn't matter." And they would wind up dropping or lessening the charges against me. They had some evidence, but they knew they didn't have enough to make it stick in court before a jury.

Without overwhelming evidence, prosecutors are always concerned that they will spend a huge amount of money taking someone to court and then lose. Then, their record suffers, too. When egos are involved, prosecutors are reluctant to take you to court and fail because that's a strike against them.

I understood that back then. I knew local prosecutors had to try to make names for themselves – they've got egos. I'll just outlast them.

After my last arrest in 1973, I got out on bond and there was a lot of discussion with the county attorney about the possibility of going to a drug rehabilitation center. I'd never had any help with my drug abuse. Nobody ever offered, I never asked for it, nor did I ever want it. But there was some discussion of them sending me, instead of prison this time, to a federal drug rehabilitation center in Kentucky. While I was out on bond, I kept my nose clean, I went to school to get a GED for a little while, I made sure I didn't get in trouble, I didn't hang around the normal spots on the streets to gather with my friends. I was very, very careful because I wanted to try somehow to beat the 25-year sentence that was coming my way for the robbery with aggravation charges I was about to face.

At the same time, I thought I might get some help with my drug abuse. It was the first time I ever wanted it. That hope didn't last long, though. While I was out on bond, they arrested me on two charges of selling drugs. They were on secret indictments, which meant the drug sales actually happened before the robbery. They caught me on camera a couple of times when I sold drugs. The same narcotics officer who was undercover when I sold the drugs arrested me on the secret indictment. I knew they had what it would take to convict me. When they arrested me on the drug charges, the county attorney dropped the prospect of my going to the drug rehabilitation center. "That ain't gonna happen," he said. "Why don't you plead guilty on the robbery charge, take the 25 years, and I'll make sure the two drug charges go away." Those charges never did make it onto my record.

We see that on TV all of the time, that kind of dealing with the issues.

So the last time I was arrested, in '73, on the robbery charge, I knew I had no way out. I knew they had an immense amount of evidence. They picked me out of a line-up. They arrested me while I had the drugs stolen from the drug store, so I pled guilty.

Robbery with aggravation carried an automatic

25 years in prison. But when you arrived in prison, you received "honor time" and "good time." Honor time was taken off the top of the sentence, which you earned by behaving yourself in prison. It was something they could take away. If they gave you eight years honor time, they could take a little bit off at a time if you screwed up. It was a carrot on a stick, a bargaining tool for them. Good time was automatically given by the governor's office. No one could touch that time given on a sentence but the governor. That immediately brought the sentence way down, so the moment I entered prison on the 25-year sentence, it went down to ten years, four months and twenty-nine days.

Then, they set up what they considered a rehabilitation program, which could include high school education, vocational education, and behavior monitoring. They gave us tests to determine what kind of risks we were. With good behavior, following the program, doing the things they wanted you to do, you could get out a great deal earlier – which I did. I did follow the program, did the things they wanted me to do.

But the real change in my life came through Christ. I'm convinced that if Christ hadn't changed me, I'd still be in prison now, caught up in the same cycle of hopelessness. In fact, I don't know of one man that I was in prison with who isn't still in prison, many of them for the third or fourth time. Or they're dead, most in violent deaths or overdoses, or they're in an insane asylum.

I had half a dozen boyhood friends of mine that died violent crime-related deaths. My friend Kenny's wife murdered him. They had an on and off relationship for a long time. His wife and one of her sons beat Kenny with a baseball bat and left him for dead in the basement of their home. But he didn't die.

A few days later, they went down to the basement to get him out and he was still alive, so they drowned him in a lake outside Des Moines. The autopsy showed that he was still alive when they threw him in because his lungs were filled with lake water.

Another friend, Joe, died of a heart attack brought on by drugs. My own brother Mike died of the same.

But in prison, we never talked about escaping the cycle we helped create. There was a lot of bitterness, a lot of conversations pitting us against them. There was a lot of kidding around to make that mundane place feel a little better, never any discussions about getting out or trying to change. It came up from time to time, but only in the way of empty talk, a way to fill the hours.

The desire to get out, to do and say what you

want, wasn't a powerful motivator. It still isn't for inmates because most men know that their situation on the outside will only be short-lived before things happen to land them back in prison. Some might fool themselves into thinking that they can get out, stay away from drugs and friends and family that are still involved in those areas. I did.

I wanted to change while I was in prison; I wanted to escape. I still messed around with drugs, though. Had I been caught, I would have been in trouble. I would have wound up doing two or three more years. Why smoke a little marijuana in prison knowing it could cost you a few more years? Simple: It's numbing. It's not just physical, it's psychological.

But like any addiction, it will take you down roads you don't want to go. It will lead you to places of no return. I got tired of the view through that window. It must be because without Christ, there's only freedom for the body; you don't sense freedom for the soul.

Chapter Six

The Hopeless Life of Prison

A lot of people ask me what prison was like. They think I'm crazy when I say that some of the easiest living I've ever known was in prison. You try and lighten up and find others who you can mess around with to have a good time; get into some trouble, but not too much. The attitude is one of, "So what if I get caught. What are they going to do? Put me in jail?"

But that doesn't mean I enjoyed it. I was stuck in a living contradiction. Life was simple, easy in a way, but completely empty and without purpose.

We didn't do drugs every day in prison, but we did get high fairly frequently. If you knew somebody with access to drugs from outside the prison – and you had the money – there were times you had as many drugs in prison as you did on the street. Certainly, it continued to be a way of life, even in prison.

I did three and a half years in Anamosa and other prison facilities. That might not sound like much time compared to inmates who do life or spend a decade or more behind bars. Some might think or wonder where I'm coming from, talking about prison life when I was in prison for only a few years.

But most all of us realize that it's not the length of the stay, or even the conditions in some instances that cause us to understand our feelings or experiences. We all know that prison starts long before incarceration.

Drugs are a prison by themselves. Like on the outside, I smoked pot in prison. I used LSD and other drugs, too. I had one friend named Billy who worked in the prison laundry with me. On Saturday mornings, we had to be at work at 8 a.m., but we only worked for a couple of hours on those days. One Saturday, we decided to drop some acid. We did it at breakfast and then went to work. We put a load of wash in the machines and sat down in the corner to talk and wait to "peak."

We were on the floor in the corner, just getting high, when the guard came back. "Hey, you guys have got to get out of here," he said. I've got to lock this place up." We mindlessly told him that we'd be up in a second. We kept talking. A few minutes later, the guard came back. "Hey, what did I tell you guys?" he asked. "You gotta get out of here. I've got to lock the laundry down."

We got up and started to stroll out of the laundry. He stopped us. "Whoa, wait a minute," he said. "Somebody's got to push that laundry cart up to the laundry room." That was the room where clean clothes and bedding were kept after they were washed and dried.

It was the middle of January in Iowa and there was a snowstorm raging outside, probably ten degrees below zero. I looked at Billy and he looked at me. "I've been here a day or two," Billy said to the guard. "I don't push no carts." Billy meant that he wasn't new to the operation, having been in a few years, and that he wouldn't be shoved around. I'd been there about a year, and the guard looked at me as if to say he understood that Billy wasn't going to push the cart, but somebody had to do it and that left me.

"Well, you know what?" I said. "It's cold outside. I don't even have any gloves. I can't push that cart. I'll freeze my hands." The cart had metal rods at either end to hold and steer while pushing. But the guard had a plan.

"I'll fix you right up," he said as he opened a cabinet drawer. Billy and I were loaded. On acid, you get different images of things. In this case, we saw the image of the guard pulling this drawer out in ultra-slow motion. The drawer came out so slowly. It seemed to take forever. Then his hand reached into the drawer and came out with a pair of bright yellow mittens. When you're on LSD, colors streak. And they're very fluorescent. This pair of yellow mittens looked like a rainbow as long as my arm coming out of the drawer. I looked at Billy and he looked at me and just started laughing. I got mad and paranoid at once, thinking he was laughing at me.

"You know," I told the guard, "I ain't pushing that cart either, man."

We left the laundry and went over to the main part of the prison. We stopped at a window looking down into the prison yard, toward the laundry. We thought the guards would be on us at any minute to pick us up and take us to the hole. We just sat there waiting, watching through the window as the snow came down. We saw the guard pushing the cart through the snow. He never did call and report us for it. We never knew why.

There aren't a lot of highlights of my time in prison that make good stories. There's no time that I say, "Well, wouldn't it be great to have pictures or a video of the time we did that?"

It's not easy for me to drag a lot of details from prison or other unpleasant experiences out into the open, either. They're comfortable where they are, lying quietly in the back of my mind. It's not uncommon for me, or people in my situation, to go through long periods of despair and all of the feelings and emotions that go with them, and not be in touch with them. It takes a lot of effort for me to really get in touch with how I felt.

Sometimes it seems like it was someone else's life. Imagine stepping out from what used to be you and seeing that now you're somebody different. It's an emotional tug of war. I am the person who went through that terrible period, who did a lot of horrible things to himself, but I'm not that person anymore. There has been a tremendous change. I've been free longer now than I was in bondage. I've been out of prison a great deal longer than I was in. I've been free of drugs longer than I was in bondage to them. So it's like sitting back and looking at a life with feelings that are buried deep in the soul – even though I know the stories and I know what I went through. Except sometimes when I get in front of a group of prisoners and talk about some of this stuff and the emotions overtake me.

Sometimes going back into prison opens them up for me again.

It might shock people who never go to prison – people who have consciences and will never commit a crime – but very few inmates ever think about the crimes they commit and how they affect their victims.

I never saw how my crimes might impact other people. There was never a feeling of regret, but there was a lack of it. I never felt like I was doing something wrong, like I was hurting someone. The absence of conscience becomes more and more pronounced as years go by, to the point where criminals don't think they've ever done anything wrong at all. As a matter of fact, I got to the point where I felt like, "you've got it and I don't, so I'm going to take yours." So you're not conscious of it. There are no feelings of guilt, no feeling of remorse.

So why change?

Beyond the prison system's plan to rehabilitate inmates is the need to change inside. Thieves, drug addicts, and all the rest of us who've been involved in the things that I've been involved with, are almost always tagged with the damning term "incorrigible." Society says they're unchangeable and the longer they're into the crime scene – the deeper they get into it – the less able they are to change.

But is your need to change really your biggest problem? To understand our greatest problem we need to first understand a few things about God.

Firstly, God is Holy, perfect and without sin.

However, we are not. Secondly, God expects us to be perfect. Jesus says in Matthew 5:48, "Be perfect, therefore, as your heavenly Father is perfect." How can that happen?

And lastly, we must all appear before the judgment throne of God on the last day. We may think our problems stem from being an alcoholic, drug addict, or criminal. Or we may think our worst problem is being in prison. But is that really true? The scriptures say in 2 Thessalonians 1:7b-8 that Jesus will return "in blazing fire with his powerful angels. He will punish those who do not know God and do not obey the gospel of our Lord Jesus." Which is worse, a destructive lifestyle or suffering eternal destruction under the wrath of a Holy and perfect God, who demands perfection from us? On that day, everything you have ever done, said, or thought will be judged. You may think that this truth is harsh or unfair. But, you must remember that any sin we commit is enormously offensive to God because He is so infinitely holy.

I realize that I have left you hanging out on a limb by explaining what your real problem is without giving you the solution. God has a solution. It is found in Jesus Christ and what He has accomplished in our place. He has done what we could never do. He led a perfect life and by that met God's demands. He also bore God's wrath on the cross in our place. How does this solve the problem? When God gives us faith, He takes our sin upon Himself, and credits us with His righteousness. As the scriptures say in Romans 5: 19, "For just as through the disobedience of the one man the many were made sinners, so also through the obedience of the one man the many will be made righteous."

It was in prison that I first heard the Gospel. An evangelical Christian group came to Anamosa on a Saturday afternoon in 1974. A friend of mine came into my cell. "Hey Sharp, you ought to go up to the auditorium to see the group that came in from the outside today," he said. "What group's that?" I asked, unimpressed. "Oh, I guess it's some Christian group from Des Moines," he answered. Still unimpressed, I told my friend that I really wasn't into the Christian thing. I told him to go if he wanted to, but I was going to pass. "You may want to reconsider," he said. "Some pretty girls came in." I asked how he knew that. "Well, I saw them when they came through the gate," he said.

So I went that afternoon. They had a band, speakers; much of what Prison Impact does in prisons now. But I went for all of the wrong reasons. I went to see the pretty girls. As I sat there, I remember hitting my friend in the shoulder and telling him, "You know, I think I'm going to go look this group up when I get back to Des Moines." I recall hearing bits and pieces of the gospel message.

I never made any connection to it and it never made a whole lot of sense to me. But it caught my attention to the degree that I said to my friend that I was going to look up the group when I got out.

But after the Christian group left Anamosa that Saturday, I didn't think about them again. Nor did I even think about Jesus Christ again, not that I even thought about Him much that day. In fact, I forgot all about Him and the group.

The closer my time came to leave prison, the more I wanted to change. I knew with my heart that I wanted to be different. I wanted to put the whole drug scene behind me. I wanted to change my friends because all of a sudden, while in prison, I realized that the people I thought were my friends all my life really were not. They were actually my enemies and didn't want me to change.

I was watching TV one afternoon on the flag, the bottom row of the cell house. There were bleachers set up in front of the TV. I was sitting there watching with another guy. He helped drive home an important message. "Hey Sharp," he said. "You know, if you don't change your attitude man, you ain't gonna have a friend left in this place." I looked at him. "What are you talking about?" I said defiantly. "You're not hanging around with us anymore," he said. "You're not using drugs, you're not playing poker anymore. You know, you're just isolating yourself."

I remember looking back at him again. "You know, first of all, I'm not convinced you're my friend," I said. "The reason I'm not convinced is that it sounds to me like you would rather have me run around with you, use drugs and get in trouble in here and spend the rest of my life in and out of this place rather than get free and not ever come back here again. It all of a sudden dawns on me that you're not my friend at all. You want me to spend the rest of my life here with you, and I don't want to do that. So you can think whatever you want to think because it doesn't matter if I have any friends in here or not. I don't want to spend the rest of my life here."

He didn't say anything. He just kept watching television.

That conversation took place not long after the Christian group showed up from Des Moines. There was something going on inside of me where I began to give serious thought to changing and wanting to change, wanting things to be different. After Anamosa, I was moved to a medium-security facility in Iowa. After you were there awhile, you could earn the privilege of coming home for a weekend and reconnecting with the community, family, and friends, that kind of thing. But on my first furlough home from prison, I had a needle back in my arm.

You might ask, what happened to the desire to change? Why would I use drugs the very day I came back to Des Moines? The only answer I have, and it's the truth, is that I was trapped. In my mind, I wanted to change, but I didn't have the willpower to say no.

When I entered prison, I had a fifth-grade education. I could barely read and I had never read a book. Prison officials asked if I wanted to get a GED. I was smart enough to know that I needed a GED to get anywhere when I got out. What a great opportunity. So I got a GED in prison. I got a vocation there, too. They blasted a horn at six o'clock every morning to get me out of bed, to try to build some discipline into my life. If I ever did get out of prison and get a job, they figured, I might be able to get there.

Those were all outward situations trying to change the inward man. God says, "My ways are different from your ways." Well, man's way to change another human being is to change his outward situation. Get an education, find a job, get a place to live, food, those elements that we need for everyday life. The hope is that the person will change inside. We don't know if the person will change or not, but we hope. We get it all wrong. God's way is to change the person inside and that change will manifest itself in his or her outward behavior.

Led by the system that's trying to change them from the outside, prisoners get it wrong, too. They learn to focus on cleaning up the outside. If they do that, maybe they don't need their insides fixed. But they need a change on the inside. Certainly, prison cleaned me up on the outside. I got a GED and a vocation while I was there. Those two things showed that I wanted to change, but what they couldn't do was change me on the inside and get me to a place where I had the strength to make the right decisions and carry through with them. Only God could do that.

Chapter Seven

Where Would I Be Now?

I've been out of prison for more than 25 years. That time and distance has allowed me to see prison life a lot more clearly. It's a life of boundaries and that's one reason why it's easy to become institutionalized. It's not that anyone – least of all, inmates – likes taking orders; but living by a routine, even in prison, becomes comfortable. You're led to your cell, let out to eat and do whatever jobs there are to do. You're told when and where to do everything. Inmates are human, they become conditioned. Once they get out, they're not used to making decisions and find that choices are very difficult to make.

Prison also appeals to inmates' need to seek approval and have someone set boundaries for them. The institutionalization happens to some people quicker than others, but if you're in prison long enough or you continue to move in and out of the system, you become institutionalized. It just becomes your way of life. Freedom is what's foreign, what you're afraid of, and what makes you feel uncomfortable.

Basically, inmates have little or no leadership once they're out. And if there's ever a vacuum for leadership, the devil will be sure to fill it. Most of us found our way into prison because we didn't have anyone in our lives to talk to about problems: drug use, the lack of direction, the things that scared us, and the hopelessness we felt. The same was true in prison. If anyone ever dared bring those things up to the guards or counselors, they'd convict themselves right away. The same is true for convicts on parole. Admitting those problems would mean complications back on the inside.

After I was in prison for a few months, two detectives came to prison from Des Moines. They called me to the Captain's office. They invited me in and asked me if I wanted a cigarette and a cup of coffee. I already had a good idea of what they were up to. They told me about some robberies that had been committed in Des Moines. They were all either robberies of drug stores or burglaries of drug stores – obviously my MO. They asked me if I would help them out.

"We'd like to get these old crimes off our

books," they said. "If you tell us which ones you committed, we'll make sure they'll never show up on your record."

"You know," I told them, "I didn't even commit the crime that I'm doing time on. Why don't you see what you can do to help me out"?

They hollered for the guard and told him what they wanted: "Get this guy out of here." I calmly smiled, said thank you and wished them well.

The emptiness of prison life also made bad news that much harder to take. I remember the day the guard brought divorce papers to me. He stuck them through the bars and turned to go. I knew what they were before I ever looked at them. I felt cursed, hurt, and full of anger. But I kept it all inside. I couldn't say anything to the other inmates because it was understood in that only-the-strong-survive environment that it would cost me my cover of toughness while I was dying inside. I couldn't tell my counselor because I knew it would show up on my psychological assessment jacket some time in the future. I just did what I knew to do and that was to shove my feelings as deeply inside me as I could and try never to think about the situation again.

Inmates still face the same lack of openness and inability to relate that I did.

Loss is what causes a lot of prisoners to cry

themselves to sleep at night, all alone in their cells. They'd never do it in front of anybody. They would never show their emotions and I wouldn't either. But in my aloneness, I cried. And the times of anger, born in that hopeless feeling, caused me to lash out at others and myself.

I had the same feelings as other prisoners: Things are never going to be any different. Why even care? Why even try to care whether they're going to be or not? Let's just live today. Let's just do what I have to do today – do what I have to do to get what I need. It's just an existence from one day to the next. We talk about goals and plans. There are no goals and plans, though – nothing to look forward to. Not even saying, "In four-and-a-half years, I'm out." You could say that, but in your heart you know that's not true. In four and a half years, I'm out and six months later, I'm back. I know the routine. I've done it. I've seen it done over and over and over again. So even if I get out, it's only going to be so I can go make myself feel good for a short period of time, then I'll come back and we'll do this whole thing again.

But God had a plan for me to get out of prison – and stay out. I was very antsy about getting out in 1976; I thought I could turn my life around on my own.

After getting cleared to leave Anamosa on

work release, I had to take a physical examination because my record showed the diagnosis of rheumatic fever which gave me a heart condition. That was part of the prison policy. If you entered prison with any type of physical problem, you had to be checked out at the University of Iowa's medical department. So when I entered prison, they cleared me. They saw that my heart was bad, but they said I was OK to get a job and participate in other activities. But when I went back to the University for release, they found that my heart valve wasn't working well. They told me they had to fix the valve and that I couldn't leave prison unless I had open-heart surgery.

Like it did in my attempt to join the Job Corps, my heart condition was again throwing a wrench into my plans.

I argued that I had just received clearance for work release. "I'm leaving prison," I said. "I don't want to get the heart valve fixed now. That's going to set me back who-knows-how-long." I tried to tell them that I could leave prison and come back in a few months and get it fixed. The doctor said it was against policy. "We can't let you out of prison unless you get your heart valve fixed," he said. So even though I didn't want to, I had to agree to have open-heart surgery and have it fixed. That set me back about six months.

Six days after surgery, two correctional officers came to transport me from the hospital in Iowa City back to prison. As they usually would, they started to slap on the handcuffs as they pulled my hands behind me. Well, my sternum had been sewn up after the doctors cut it open to work on my heart. I could feel my chest stretch as they put my hands behind me. It was incredible pain! I dropped to my knees. The nurse was there. She screamed at them: "What are you doing?" she yelled. "You don't have to handcuff him!"

They told her I was a criminal and they had to take me back to prison. "Why do you think you have to handcuff him?" she shot back. "He's just had open-heart surgery. Where do you think he's going to go?"

They cuffed my hands in front of me and took me back to prison where they put me in an infirmary cell. I remember being there all alone, coming down off a lot of the painkillers I was on for the surgery and recuperation. I was scared to death. The primary reason I was scared was because I knew that nobody in that prison cared whether I lived or died. There I was locked in this little cell, in the row of infirmary cells in the basement. In a normal cell, there would be a lot of activity with guards and other prisoners passing by. In the infirmary, there's not a lot of activity;

you saw very few people.

All by myself. It's not like a hospital. There wasn't really an easy way to even get to a hospital if something happened. I just had this incredible feeling of being scared. That was one of the scariest times of my life. And that fright was accompanied only by the feeling of being alone.

Healing up after surgery, I eventually left the penitentiary to go to a minimum-security facility, which was the next step in release back to the community. One of the things that you could earn while you were there was a furlough home for the weekend. That was one way that the institution could find out how well you were going to do in re-entering society.

I often think about how easy it would be for me to still be in the cycle of drugs, crime, and prison. The lure, the raw reality that nothing had changed told me to go ahead, live for the moment at hand. I would take my furloughs to my mother's house and my brothers and others nearby were still involved in drugs. When I came home on my first furlough in '76 and got high, nothing was different. After three years of prison, I was back doing the things that had always taken me down the same road to nowhere. I still didn't understand what I really had to do to change.

On parole that year, I kept myself busy with a

needle in my arm, getting high regularly. It wasn't long before I began carrying a gun again and getting involved in criminal activity.

Just carrying the gun, of course, would have been a parole violation. Between that and the drugs, I figured there was a pretty good chance I'd be caught. At times, I was paranoid about getting caught. Other times, I just didn't care. I didn't care because it was just a matter of time anyway. What's the point of all this? I used to think. In prison, I spent all of those months thinking about how wonderful it was going to be when I was released. I was going to get a good job. I was going to get my family back and see my kids again. I would have some kind of normal life. Only, when I was released from prison, I headed right back where I came from. In the same scene, with the same people, doing the same things. I was still trapped.

Drug addiction for me has been much more mental than physical. I seemed to get over the physical part of it quickly. I shot heroin and used other drugs on and off for many years. And, like so many other inmates on parole, I had fallen back to my old way of life using drugs and running with the wrong people, doing all the wrong things. It was just a matter of time before it all would fall apart.

That prospect hit home when my parole officer

very candidly told me that if I didn't get full time gainful employment I was going to have to return to prison. Parole revocation.

I had been out of Anamosa for nearly a year. I'd had jobs, thirty days at one place, a couple of weeks at another. My parole officer told me to get a job and stick with it or I was on my way back to the minimum-security facility. That was one of the rules of parole: You either had to be in school full-time or show progress in full-time employment. Besides my short-term jobs, I went to vocational school for a little while, too. For the majority of that first year out, I was drifting from job to job, and looking like I was headed for trouble. My parole officer could see that. "There's nothing consistent here," he said. "You're on a slow boat going nowhere. If you don't get it together, it's back to prison for you."

At that point, I made a decision that I had to get a job. I looked in the paper, saw an ad for a carpentry job at the hospital, and went for an interview. I didn't know it at the time, but it was part of God's plan. It seemed like the right job for me. The thing that stood out about it was that it was in the carpentry shop. I had experience working as a carpenter and had received vocational training in carpentry while I was in prison. So it seemed to be a perfect fit, a job that my experience gave me a chance to get. Plus, the hospital wasn't very far from home. I didn't have a car. It was on the bus route and it was within walking distance if I had to. It was a county hospital, too, so I was a little familiar with it because being from a poor welfare family, you have a lot of contact with a county hospital – it's the only place you can go.

I really wanted that job, but I didn't pray for it. I didn't know how to do that and I didn't think then that prayer would make much of a difference. Whether or not I would get that job had already been determined in God's plan, though. I just could not have understood how.

Chapter Eight

The Plan At Work

The job interview at the hospital in Des Moines would be the most important thing that happened to me after I got out of Anamosa. I had no way of knowing that at the time, though.

I was afraid. While in prison, I began to really consider whether I wanted to spend the rest of my life there on the installment plan. There were many inmates who had accepted that they would. I knew that if I didn't find some permanent work, and soon, I'd be in trouble again. It wouldn't matter how much I wanted to change, I was proving that I couldn't.

I didn't have long to turn things around, either, just a month or so. Find the right job? I thought I might have just as much luck shedding my old skin and finding a new one. "Who would ever want to give me a chance?" I wondered.

But I was lucky to find the newspaper ad – at least I thought it was luck. Carpentry was the only trade I knew. I answered the ad, but there was so much more than my qualifications or even simple luck at work. God had a plan.

When I went in for the interview, I saw the mother of an old friend of mine. The woman came up to me. "Ronnie, is that you?" she asked. "It's Alma, Mike's mom."

Mike was an old friend of mine. We used to do drugs together in the early '70s. He had died in a motorcycle accident just months before and I was a pallbearer at his funeral. My friends and I always knew there was something different about Mike's mother, but I had no idea what she did, let alone that she worked at the hospital. When I saw her there, I told her I had applied for the carpentry shop job and that I was waiting to talk with someone in the personnel department.

"Oh, OK," she said. "Well, I'll be back to see you in a few minutes." She left quickly and went down the hall.

She wasn't gone long and seemed to be on her way somewhere else when she came back.

"It was nice to see you again," she said. "Hope to see you again soon."

Then, the personnel manager called me in and there was a guy in her office with her. It was the maintenance department supervisor. The three of us talked for a little while and I soon understood that I was going to get the job. But the supervisor told me exactly how he felt.

"I'm going to give you this job," he said. "I know your record. I know where you've been. I know what your life's been, but I'm going to give you a chance. I'm only going to give you one chance, though."

"OK," I said. And I was hired.

What I didn't know was that before they called me into that personnel office, Mike's mother had gone in there and talked to the personnel manager. The way she was different – what my friends and I only bothered to see on the surface – was that she was a Christian. The personnel manager was a Christian, too. They knew each other and shared their faith. So after Mike's mother saw me in the hall, she went in and talked to the personnel manager. "I think we ought to hire that guy," Mike's mother told the manager. "I think God might be doing something here."

I didn't even know the whole story of any of this until I had been working at the hospital awhile, and after I was saved. But God had all of this worked out. He put all of this together for me.

How did He do it? He often works behind the scenes. Another thing I didn't know about was that when I was a pallbearer at Mike's funeral, Alma watched the six of us take Mike's coffin from the hearse and bring it to the gravesite. The six of us were all into drugs, using and abusing our lives. As we moved the coffin, she prayed for all of us, asking God for our salvation, she told me later. From her prayers and His grace, four of us have come to know Christ.

We rarely pay attention to this Unseen Presence that is at work setting up these situations for us, bringing other people into play. Why does God do that? He does it because He loves His sheep.

In case you wonder what it is that makes people Christians, it's not always a clap of thunder or a bolt of lightning. I know those things happen, but they're kind of rare. I never spent much time wondering about the process. Before I went to prison, I just thought I didn't need Christianity, or God, in my life. Even after I got out of Anamosa, I was content to live by my own rules. They may not have worked out very well for me, but they were all I knew.

The time in prison and more years of incarceration strung together in local jails throughout Iowa showed me that I was on the wrong road, but, like most ex-cons who try to make it after prison, I was trapped. I kept up the same behavior because I was in what I now know is a "cycle" of drugs, crime, violence and poverty. I was locked in this cycle of bondage, and it felt as though it was impossible to break out. You're desensitized. There's a lack of conscience, a lack of remorse. What you do know is, "I don't have it and you do, so I'm going to take yours."

Prison can clean you up on the outside and it did that for me. I got the GED, a vocation, but it's still an empty existence, a long road to nowhere. Even when you get out, things still seem hopeless. The only difference is that nobody's making all of your decisions for you. Drugs offered an easy path off that road – in prison and out. They were an easy way to escape. They let me numb my feelings of aloneness, despair and shame.

My criminal activities and prison time also helped make my hot temper hotter. Even after I got out, I continued to have outbursts of anger – not as violent as they once were, but still explosive. I continued to have feelings that I couldn't be of value to other people.

After God saved me, I understood and accepted right from the get-go God's embrace of me and my value to Him. But it took me a few years to see that others could accept me, and that they could have my best interests in mind. After all these years, I still struggle at times when I don't feel able to trust others. They must have some ulterior motive.

They must be up to something that will come back to haunt me later. Those feelings have lessened over the years, but even now, 25 years since my conversion and more than that since I left prison, I still have a few of those issues to work through.

The past dies hard – and the change that was coming behind the scenes still hadn't come while I was working at the hospital. No matter what God was doing for me, I didn't recognize it during the first few months there.

So the hospital job wasn't a cure-all. I often tell men and women getting out of prison that you might not find the job you want right away, but you will find the job you need.

A few months into the job, I was proving that I wasn't a model employee – my old habits were back on track. Along with a co-worker, I drank tequila most of the day. We cut lumber with radial arm saws, made cabinets, tables and other wooden items. We worked around all of this dangerous machinery, sipping tequila all day and smoking marijuana. That was our everyday routine, and it fit the pattern I had always known.

I had gotten more antisocial during that time, too, and I wasn't really conscious that it was happening at all. I remember my older brother, Mike, who had already been in prison three or four times, stopped me on a flight of stairs at our mom's home. I was coming up, he was coming down and he stopped me. He looked at me and said, "You know, you need to find yourself a friend, someone to talk to, or you're not going to make it." I had lost all trust in anyone and it drove me deeper within myself.

My brother didn't know Christ, but it was almost a prophetic statement that he wasn't even aware of. Some years later, I asked him if he remembered the conversation. He didn't.

Within a few weeks of my brother's assessment, I was invited to a church service. It was called a "Sunday Night Jesus Gathering." It was the sort of event that took place in the mid- to late-1970s. They had a Christian rock band made up of people who had come out of drugs and the lifestyle I had been familiar with. The country had been going through a "Jesus Revolution," a renewal of faith and love for God, that seemed to bypass me.

It was the sort of meeting we had in prison, much like the one I went to almost two years before I got out. I hadn't planned to go to this one either, but one of my sisters asked me to go. She had been saved. I knew nothing about it. She hardly understood it herself, but out of her love and concern for me, she brought up the meeting. "Hey Ronnie, I've heard about this Christian meeting every Sunday night," she said. "There are a lot of people there like you who've been involved in some of the things that have been a struggle for you. If you'd ever like to go, I'll go with you." My response was, "What do you mean, like me?" She explained that she didn't mean anything by it and I said, "Sure, I'll go with you sometime."

I was high on drugs when I went to the Des Moines gathering. We listened to the same story I had heard in prison. You know, "Jesus loves you. He has a plan for your life." All of a sudden, I see that it's the same band that came to Anamosa. After I left prison and went home to Des Moines, I was going to look them up, but I never did. I forgot all about them.

But there I was two years later, at this Jesus gathering with the same band, the same group of people, telling me the same thing. And as I sat there, it hit me. I realized something I didn't understand in prison, that I was a sinner in need of a savior. I could leave that building the same man that I was when I came in. Or I could leave that night a changed person. Nobody told me that. I just knew that. Obviously, God was informing me, somehow giving me that information. Thank God for His grace. And I went down to the front.

A young guy comes up and he says, "Did you come down here to receive Jesus Christ?" I said, "Buddy, I came down here for everything you've got because I'm the neediest man you've ever met."

Since then, I have come to realize that the scriptures do not talk about receiving Jesus Christ but about believing in the good news of Jesus Christ. In other words, the gospel is not an invitation but a proclamation. God uses that proclamation to call His sheep unto himself. In John 6:44, Jesus said, "No one can come to me unless the Father who sent me draws him, and I will raise him up at the last day."

The only thing I knew about Jesus was that there was this man named Jesus Christ who died on this cross. I knew little or nothing about Him. But God supernaturally was revealing himself to me by regenerating me and giving me the gift of faith.

I can't explain it, other than saying that the beginning of it came in prison when I saw and heard the same message and that it started to hit home when my brother said to me, "You need to find a friend, someone you can talk to, or you're not going to make it." And over the next few weeks, things began to snowball. Well, this guy gave me a Bible that night and he pointed out what to read. "Read the book of John," he said. "Don't go to the rest of it. Just read the book of John because I think it will make sense to you now."

I began to read. I got up the next morning and instead of getting ready for work by smoking some pot, I sat down and read that Bible. I started reading the book of John. And when I looked in the mirror that morning, I saw somebody different in that mirror than I'd seen the day before. It was like somebody else was living inside of me and looking out through my eyes. I mean, I saw the world differently. Overnight! I had a different attitude. I was thinking about different things. I had hope for the first time since I had been a young boy. I was a changed man, from one day to the next.

I took the Bible they'd given me at the altar call to work the next day. I was sitting in the back of the room on my lunch break reading it when my boss walked in.

"What are you doing there?" he asked.

"Oh, I'm reading this book," I said. "It's a Bible."

"Yeah?" he said, "You can't be a Christian and work here."

"Really, why is that?" I asked.

"I've tried," he said.

"What do you mean you've tried?" I was confused; I didn't know what to think.

"I've tried to be a Christian and work here," he said. "This is not an easy environment to try to live as a Christian."

"You know, you might be right," I said. "I don't know much about it, but I'm going to give it a shot."

Chapter Nine

Decisions and Responsibilities

After I told my boss, Darrell, that I was going to give the Christian life a shot no matter how difficult it might be, my life changed. I mean, changed radically. But it wasn't easy because there were many areas in my life where it was still hard to follow God's will. The gal that I had been seeing for months was still in the drug scene and didn't seem to want to change and I needed to break away from anything and anyone that wasn't consistent with my new life. Many of my friends and even members of my family were in the same dangerous scene. As much as I cared for them, I knew I had to be careful not to fall back into the trap from which I had managed to escape.

Personal responsibility is so important. Many people expect that believing in the gospel automatically fixes all of their problems. Our greatest problem, which is salvation from the wrath of God, is met in Christ. However, the daily changes of the Holy Spirit's sanctifying work has just begun. Up until the time I believed and traded in my tequila and drugs for Bible-reading, I was not responsible to myself, to God, to anyone. That irresponsibility, obviously, affected others. But the fact that I could change had just as dramatic an impact.

The proof hit me in waves. Darrell came to talk to me again a few weeks after our brief conversation about the hospital not being a good place to try to live as a Christian. "You know, I've been watching you," he said. "I want you to know something. Do you remember that night that you were at the Jesus Gathering and you answered the altar call to give your life to Jesus Christ? I was there."

I was shocked. "You were there?" I asked. "What were you doing there?"

His daughter sang in the band at the Jesus Gathering. "Yeah, I was sitting behind you," he said. "I watched the whole thing. And I've been watching you since then and I've come to the conclusion that you can be a Christian and work here. I'm going to give it a shot; I'll try too. I just rededicated my life to Christ. Now I'm going to serve him – as I've watched you serve Him." So, as God was changing my life, He was using my example to change another life, too.

Actually, there were more lives headed for change. I was fixing a broken door in the hospital one morning. A patient was sitting nearby in the hallway. As I was working on the lock, I looked out of the corner of my eye and as our eyes met, he began to cry. I stopped and put my hand on his shoulder and asked him what was wrong. He told me that he had just found out that he had cancer and that he was dying.

My heart fell into my shoes. I said I have no idea what you might be going through, but I know if you give your life to Jesus Christ and really mean it that you'll be with him when you die (as I have said before, we are not saved by anything we do or decide but by what God has done). I asked him if he had ever made this kind of decision and he said that he had in the Los Angeles county jail a few months before. He was traveling through town when he got sick and came to the county hospital. I began to visit him on my breaks and prayed and read the Bible with him.

He was released from the hospital a few days later but didn't have anywhere to go. I arranged for him to live at a public shelter in Des Moines and I went to visit him when I could. He told me one day that he had received a letter from his sister in

Las Vegas and that she asked him to come and live with her and her family until he passed away. He asked me what I thought and I told him that if it was me, that if I had family that wanted to be with me in my last days, I would go. A few days later, I took him to the bus station and he was off to Las Vegas. I received a letter from his sister months later and in it, she thanked me and told me that her brother had told her before he died that I was the only friend he ever had.

How do you live for more than forty years and never feel like you had a friend? I'm not sure I know, but I've come to find out that one of my greatest fears, that all men have ulterior motives, is not true, and God does provide the friendship we need through others.

Everything seemed to be changing radically. It was like this invasion of God came in such a way that I changed without even trying.

That was an important message of what my faith could do, but like the old saying goes, God must have been telling me, "You ain't seen nothing yet."

There I was with so many strikes against me, I figured I'd never have a normal life. I was still on parole; I had 20 years in the drug scene in Iowa, an incredible history of a life of crime, and a police file that was probably two inches thick. I was out of prison just over a year after the robbery with aggravation conviction. I had a history of burglary in Des Moines. Why should anyone trust me with anything important? But God had many people show me that He loved me and had a plan for me – a plan much bigger than I could ever dream of.

And then God showed me how anything was possible through faith. One of my jobs at the carpentry shop had been to call a commercial locksmith to "key" locks or make keys for us. I usually spent a day with the locksmith when he came to the hospital. I'd show him the individual locks and help in other ways. Then my supervisor shocked me. "You know, I think we need a locksmith of our own instead of calling the lock company all the time," he said. "Would you be interested if we trained you?"

"Sure," I said. So they sent me to school and I learned to be a locksmith. Here I am, this old burned-out drug addict who is fresh out of prison. Still on parole and I'm not just making the keys to the hospital locks and keying all the locks, I've got master keys to every lock in the hospital. The drug cabinets, the pharmaceutical laboratories, I had all of the keys.

God's got such a sense of humor. Scripture says He takes the abase things of this world to confound the wise. It doesn't make any sense, but when God works in people's lives, it doesn't have to make sense from a logical perspective.

The hospital wasn't meant to be my only calling, though. God showed me there were many other locks that He needed me to unlock for Him.

After I had become a Christian, my ex-wife was still heavily involved in drugs and the whole lifestyle. There was still a significant amount of violence around her home. For the first time in my life, I saw my responsibility as a parent, as a father. I took my ex-wife to court and sued her for custody of our daughters.

They were three-years-old and one-year-old when I went to prison. At the time I went to court, they were nine and seven. I hardly knew them and they hardly knew me. I certainly didn't know how to be a father.

I was paying child support and had visiting privileges with them – on the weeks that I could find them at their mother's home. I could see that my daughters were already entering a hopeless situation, that cycle of drugs, crime and possibly prison, that would affect their whole lives. I realized that I was the only way of escape for them. It was my responsibility.

I didn't know how to be a father, how to be a parent. I didn't know the first thing about it. I hadn't lived with my daughters for years. Try to imagine: One day, you're living alone; the next, you have two little girls living with you that you're responsible for and you don't know the first thing about it. What a trip!

But it all came about after I had a conversation with God. "I don't know the first thing about all of this and I'm scared," I told Him. "I don't know how to be a father. I'm just learning how to be responsible, but if this is what You want me to do, this is what I'll do if You promise to help me." Of course, he did.

I had incredible feelings of inadequacy. There was even a time early on, when I didn't want to do it. For the first time in my life, I was free. I could look out the window and see that there were opportunities for me. Now, all of a sudden, I'm going to be strapped to two little girls. So there was a part of me that didn't want to do it, that didn't want to take the responsibility and wanted to serve my new opportunities and myself. But, at the same time, I knew that it was my responsibility. Part of being a parent is sacrificing your life for your children, even sacrificing the things that you might want to do with your life.

Those were all new concepts for me. They're certainly biblical concepts. It's that amazing lesson and gift that the Lord gave us. Jesus came to Earth to die for our sins, to give us, His children, eternal life. I could read that and I could connect with the reading of that, but living that example was something else.

So once again, I was faced with conscious choices of what was right and what was wrong. I could see that even though it was going to hurt like hell, I had to do the right thing.

The court fight to gain custody lasted about six months in 1979. My ex-wife didn't even show for the hearing, which is how I won custody. I had already proven that she was still involved in the drug scene and that she was still in bad shape, but she could have won custody. "If Mary had come today and told me that she wanted help and that she wanted to change, I wouldn't be taking the kids out of the home and giving them to Ron," the judge told my lawyer.

But she didn't come. The girls think — and I think they're probably right — that she made a conscious choice, that she knew she couldn't be what they needed at that point and decided not to come.

She tried to change. There was even a short time when she came to church on Sundays. I never wanted to be married to her again, but in those few months, God seemed to be doing something in her life that forced me to think about "what if?" Does God want me remarried to Mary? Can she change?

Can things be different? I wrestled with all of that for several months. Then she chose to go a different way. I didn't think about it much after that.

Complicating the matter was the fact that Mary was one of three sisters that married three brothers all around the same time. Two of my brothers are still married to her two sisters. My brother and his wife, her sister, gave their lives to Christ at that time. So she saw all of this, she heard the message and saw what God was doing, but obviously made a conscious decision then that she wasn't going to respond favorably to what she heard, what she saw.

Others in my family, including my mother who is deceased now, committed their lives to Christ. God came into my family like a whirlwind and whoever decided to bend a knee He saved. I have seen Him do this many times over the years in other families.

As I look back now, I can see how difficult it was for my mother to handle my dad's death. It was hard on her to have so many kids and no husband to help. We made it harder, too, when we chose lives of crime. For a while, she made jail visits to three sons behind bars.

Obviously, she made bad choices for her own life, but just as He did in mine, God brought her to a place of change and faith.

Chapter Ten

Staying the Course

The Holy Spirit gave me the gift of faith at a church in Des Moines called the New Life Center. In the 1960s and early '70s, it was also a Christian community – as it is today. People formed Christian communities in those days by committing themselves to each other and to their shared desire to serve Christ. Members of each community made all kinds of sacrifices, like giving up financial resources and professional opportunities, to be part of the communities. My altar call experience was so strong, I joined the community.

There was a strong sense of sacrifice, change, and service, and for someone like myself who came out of an incredible amount of rebellion that led to destruction, it was a place where a person could learn many of the disciplines that I hadn't learned in my earlier years, such as authority. I lived in the community for several years and God used the many people at the center to bring much needed change to my life.

On Saturdays, we went to a mall and handed out fliers that told stories about Christ, or gave out a monthly newspaper that we printed. Or we'd go downtown and just stand on street corners, two or three of us, and talk to people about Jesus Christ. And then late Saturday afternoon, we'd all meet for devotions and have dinner together. Then we would talk about what happened that day: "What did Jesus do today?" Like the Bible tells us Jesus did with his disciples. He sent them out two by two and they came back and they began to tell him all that God had done. It was such an exciting experience to be involved in God's work in the lives of others and I learned many valuable things in those days.

After lunch one Saturday, I was sitting in a living room where we had gathered after a day of telling people about Jesus. I looked across the room and there was a girl there from my past life. I was so excited about seeing her there. The guy who had led her to Jesus Christ that day told how he had done that and she gave a little testimony. Afterward, I went up to her and said, "Hi." We hugged and we were so excited that she had come to know the Lord. I told her that we had a prayer meeting every Tuesday night and that if she wanted to come, I would pick her up. "I'd love to come," she said.

We went to the next prayer meeting and sat down in the back. We weren't too far into the meeting when she asked if I wouldn't mind taking her home. "You mean now?" I asked. "Yeah," she said. "I'd forgotten. I really need to get home." We left and pulled up in front of her house. She asked me to wait a few minutes because she wanted to see if her brother was home. He wasn't.

"My brother's up at this bar," she said motioning up the street. "Would you mind dropping me off there?"

I knew that wasn't a good idea. "I'll drop you off there," I told her. "But are you sure that's what you want to do? It's not consistent with the decision you made to follow Christ." She said she'd be OK, that she just wanted to talk to her brother for a few minutes. We drove to the bar and I parked in the lot across the street. She looked at me and asked a very simple question that would have a huge impact.

"Do you want to come in for a few minutes?"

In seconds, so many thoughts crossed my mind: I could go into the bar, have a couple of beers, and probably wind up sleeping with that girl. I hadn't been with a woman for quite some time and it all sounded like it would feel real good. All of this went on inside my mind – it was a very intense span of a few moments. I told her it really wasn't what I wanted for my life, knowing that it was likely to lead me down a path I just didn't want to go. She got out of the truck and went into the bar. I couldn't get my truck going fast enough to head back to that prayer meeting. When I got there, I literally ran up to the school where the meeting was being held and sat down in the back. It was like a bag of rocks was taken off my shoulders.

I don't know what happened to the girl. That was the last I ever saw of her.

One afternoon at the New Life Center, I became agitated and upset after being told by the leaders to do something that I didn't want to do. I was still early in the process of learning that we don't live our lives in a vacuum and that there are lines of authority that provide safe places.

I was living in a house for men – there were probably six of us there – and that evening, I decided to leave and run. I'd had a big disagreement with the man who was kind of the big brother of the house. I had grown tired of being around others all of the time. It was hard after being so antisocial for so many years.

But out of something that seemed so drastic, so final, God provided a new beginning.

When I left the New Life Center, it was early

evening in Des Moines. I drove to the apartment complex where my brother and his family lived. I didn't know where else to go. The hilly street in front of the complex, Fleur Drive, runs right into the heart of Des Moines. From outside the city, where the apartment was, the road crests before sliding down into the Des Moines River valley.

I pulled into the parking lot. It was night and I could stand by my truck and see all the way into the valley. The city lights shined brightly, like diamonds dropped on a bed of dark soil. I was feeling angry. I was feeling rebellious, wanting to just quit, and scared about it all. I was scared of all of these feelings that I thought had been dealt with: My doubts about faith, my self esteem and value to society. These old feelings of worthlessness, of being alone in the world, all of a sudden began to rush up and fill my head.

As I stood there, I could see the lights of the city. I remembered the Scripture of Christ's journey into the wilderness for 40 days. Satan tries his best to tempt Him. "You bow down to me and serve me and I'll give you all of that," Satan said to Jesus as he showed him a view of the world. It was as if he said that to me, too, right there on that spot. And I said to him, out loud, "It's not what I want." As quickly as he came, he was gone.

It was one of those times that God used my

decision as such a growth spurt in my life. My life continued to change for the better and my faith was renewed and deepened after that moment. It was the sort of temptation that hits all of us. The devil says, "Go ahead, just chuck it all. You don't need this. You can have a lot more fun in life!" That's something that other men and women continually face when they get out of prison.

Just because you're saved, just because you believe in Christ as your Savior, doesn't mean that temptation ever goes away. A commitment to faith is part of a long journey that lasts the rest of your life – and beyond.

But the great question is, where would I be today if I had said, "OK, lets do that for a few months"? Sounds great, you know. Go back to drugs and, boy, I ain't had a woman for several months now and that sure sounds like it'd feel good, too. Where would I be today, more than 20 years later, if I had said, "Yes"? Probably not in a book about God's ability to change a person's life.

What is "all that" that Satan offered? It's the things of the world that draw us to be a friend of the world and Jesus clearly tells us that you cannot be a friend of His and a friend of the world at the same time. That, of course, means different things to different people. One of the challenges of being a Christian is to have the kind of relationship with

Christ that you're able to identify the value of the things that Satan offers compared to the peace and joy that we find accepting our part in God's kingdom, rather than the kingdom of this world.

The road to salvation gave me a chance to prove what I had known was in my heart, that I wanted to be different. I wanted to end the drug use, I wanted out of the crime – to cut out all of the bad areas of my life. But I was still trapped in that horrible cycle of drugs, crime, violence, and poverty – until I was saved and began making conscious decisions to follow Christ.

There are plenty of examples of how those decisions send people in opposite directions.

It wasn't long after that when my pastor came and asked me, "Do you think you'd ever want to go back to prison and preach to prisoners?" I thought about it, but I'd had enough of prisons and I'd had enough of prisoners for that matter. Nobody on the outside knows what it's like to live in a prison with a thousand men with attitude problems. "I don't really care if they stay there the rest of their lives," I told the pastor. I was free and that's all that counted for me right then. God took about six months to change my heart and get me to where I not only knew he wanted me to go back to prison to tell my story, but I wanted to go as well.

I remember the first time I went back, too.

I went to the prison at Newton, Iowa, which then was the Riverview Release Center. I met with the warden who had been in charge when I was a prisoner there. I called him one day. "Ron Matthews," I said, "I'd like to come down to talk with you about what's happened in my life. Would you give me a short time to come down and talk with you?" He was willing and we set up a time for me to come down.

I sat in front of his desk and shared my testimony with him, telling him how Christ had changed my life. Then, I was still on parole and not long out of prison. He listened to me, didn't say a word. Even when I was finished, he didn't have much to say. "Well, what do you want me to do?" he said.

I told him I wanted to teach a Bible study in the prison. I was ready to argue the refusal I expected, but I wasn't ready for the answer he gave.

"Well, when do you want to come?" he asked.

It was unheard of that a man just out of prison, still on parole, could go back in to prison that way. The following week, I started to teach a Bible study and I did that for six years. I traveled the eighty-five-mile round trip every week for six years to teach the Bible study. I was eventually asked to be the chaplain of the prison.

I was surprised when Ron asked me to be

chaplain. He began to tell me what a good job I'd been doing. "Ron, we need to hire a new chaplain for the prison," he said, "and we'd like you to consider the position." I couldn't believe that someone in his position saw me as valuable enough to be a colleague and not just another person who wanted to come to prison.

It was a huge experience in my believing how valuable I was to God in Christ and how He was causing others to see me that way, too.

Even before that happened, there was another moment in my life that would shape my commitment to God's plan to change the lives of prisoners. I was still a volunteer teacher at the prison when Chuck Colson came to town in 1979. He brought his just-released film, *Born Again*. He had just started Prison Fellowship Ministries a few years before that. Primarily, their work was on the East Coast. He was traveling around the country with the new movie, and he would come to places like Des Moines and invite anyone who was interested in or connected with prison ministry to premiere showings of his movie. I was one of those people.

I already had started a not for profit organization of my own called Freedom Ministries. I had a lot of grandiose ideas about building this national prison ministry, but as I sat there and listened to Chuck, I heard his heart, saw his vision, and his mission for Prison Fellowship. I knew that I probably could accomplish a whole lot more with my life if I hooked up with Chuck. So I did. Along with a couple of other men, I spearheaded Prison Fellowship's work here in Iowa. I worked with Prison Fellowship as a volunteer for the next seven years.

They hired a director for Iowa and I continued my work as a volunteer, teaching Bible study, speaking, and working in other areas for Prison Fellowship. Then, in 1986, they hired me to be state director of Kansas.

My daughters and I packed up and moved to the Kansas City area and started a new life together as I worked as state director for eight years. I was promoted in 1993, to be regional director in charge of the ten states in the Northwest.

One of the interesting things about the regional director position is that I was an ex-convict with a GED that he had to work so hard to get, supervising people with college degrees. When I entered prison at twenty-five, I had a fifth-grade-education level. I could hardly read. I had never read a book. But God's got such an incredible sense of humor. He proved once again that it doesn't matter what this world produces, it matters what He produces.

Where else does that kind of thing happen

other than in the kingdom of God?

A personal note from Ron Matthews, former treatment director, Riverview Release Center:

When I had an opportunity to help authorize [Ron's] re-entry into our facility to lead Bible studies while still on parole, I arranged to do so. He faithfully came to lead these activities and to eventually work for Prison Fellowship. Ron never let us down, in fact he made a real difference in a very challenging setting. I enjoyed both his success and his friendship as we worked together on projects with other dedicated local volunteers.

Few will dispute prisons are a place where it is difficult to retain and strengthen your beliefs. Ron gave many inspiration and assurance that our efforts were indeed meaningful. I personally found the spirit of the Lord in his positive perspective and sense of purpose. I know that is why he reached so many of the individuals he returned to minister to and through.

He exhibits a personal power that can only come from one who has truly embraced the Lord with his soul!

Chapter Eleven

Reaping What We Sow

My work with Chuck Colson and Prison Fellowship has always been very rewarding. In so many ways, it helped me lay the foundation for my work now. I learned a great deal about the needs and joys of ministry work and, of course, the difficult things such as sacrificing our own lives for His call to the ministry. I spent a significant amount of time with the organization. But the way that I joined Prison Fellowship is a story worth telling. It will help show that God's plan doesn't always work out the way we would like or follow the timetable we would like. But it all makes sense when we step back and look at the logic and wisdom of what God does with our lives.

When I met Chuck and saw his movie *Born Again*, he talked about his vision and the mission he felt that he had from God to start Prison

Fellowship. His passion for prison ministry was so compelling, two other men and I worked as volunteers to help get things going for a Prison Fellowship office in Des Moines in the early days before there was money to pay for a staff.

Then, the organization decided to hire a state director. In the interview process, I met Mel Goebel, then Prison Fellowship's director for the state of Nebraska. Mel's faith journey is an incredible Christian story, a powerful testimony to God's grace. He is, in fact, the author and subject of *The Unseen Presence*, the second book in Prison Impact's 70 x 7 series, and a wonderful brother in Christ.

Mel and a businessman affiliated with Prison Fellowship at that time came to Des Moines and interviewed three or four people, including me, for the new position. Mel and the other man felt that it was me that God was calling to be state director for Iowa. The people in Prison Fellowship's human resource department didn't see it that way, though. They hired one of the other men who had helped in seeding the ministry and it was one of the earliest blows dealt to me in my ministry work.

As if that wasn't hard enough, the man who was hired left the post after a few years to return to being a church pastor. When they hired his replacement, I was passed over again as they hired another candidate from another state and brought him to Iowa.

Because I had helped to seed the ministry around the state, I knew many of the volunteers and chaplains very well, of course. I had good working relationships with them and they were up in arms about Prison Fellowship hiring someone else. They felt that I was the guy who should be hired. They wrote letters to Chuck Colson, angry letters.

I had to stop them. I reached as many of the people who were trying to support me as I could. "You know, if God wants me to be the state director, I will be," I said. "It's not something I have to fight about to make happen. To be honest with you, I think that I will be the director one day. It just might not be this time." So I calmed the situation down.

When the new director arrived in Des Moines, I met with him and told him what I'd been doing in my volunteer work for the organization. I wanted him to know that I was ready to help him be all that God wanted. I gave him a list of different things I'd done, but told him I would do whatever he needed. We became very good friends and did a lot of things over the next couple of years as co-workers that helped make Prison Fellowship effective in the state of Iowa.

Then in 1986, Prison Fellowship needed a

director for the state of Kansas. Because of my continuing volunteer work with the ministry, the personnel people asked me to interview for the position. Soon, I was hired as the Kansas state director and they moved us – my daughters and me – to Kansas City.

My daughters and me. That reference, that simple phrase, might not sound that important. But it is. It's a description that I probably didn't think too much about after I got married and after each of them was born. I didn't think of myself as a father, at least not more than in name only. I loved them as much as I knew how to love. I just didn't know what a father really was or did.

I had to learn. My daughters had to teach me.

The one thing I did know when I sought custody of them in 1979 was that I had to break the cycle that my children were in. They were living with their mother and there were drugs, crime and violence around the home. They didn't have many role models around them to show them how to make good decisions. Not that I had all of the answers, but I was learning what was right.

I try not to lead people to think that I was so good and my former wife was so bad, but God was stabilizing my life and was showing me the real meaning of life. I do know that, with Christ's guidance and help, I had an opportunity to be used by Him and to break the cycle that I had helped create in my daughters' lives. It's important for prisoners to understand that they're not just saving their own lives when they put drugs and crime aside. Each decision has an impact on so many other lives, too.

Children look to their parents first to see examples of how to live. You can be selfish and say that the children aren't your responsibility. But you are responsible. Would you want their image of you to be a drugged-out shell of a person, or the proud and involved parent who teaches them the things that will keep them from making the same bad decisions that will lead them down paths that they don't want to go down – the ones that you and others have traveled?

But don't think it will be all smiles and laughs. That's not the nature of parenthood. It wasn't for me. But I wouldn't have traded my job as a father for anything.

My daughters Mindy and Sam were nine and seven when they came to live with me. They didn't know me, I didn't know them. I didn't know anything about being a parent. I did it unwillingly at first only because I knew I was their only escape from a devastating cycle. But I knew then that it was the greatest thing I would do with my life. I also figured it would be the hardest.

In most cases, children of divorced or separated parents are better off with the mother because men are not equipped with what I would call mothering instincts. Women can get jobs and support kids, but they have these built-in mothering instincts that men don't have. It was always hard for me because I didn't know what they were thinking. In their teenage years, they seemed to wake up as different persons every day.

My oldest daughter, Mindy, was a very angry young girl when she came to live with me.

For the first couple of years, she frequently got into fistfights or other big arguments with kids in school. We had a talk one day. I told her one thing that seemed to have an impact and help her reshape her thinking. I told her that prior to my coming to know Christ, I was a very angry person. Like her, I had been putting myself in the wrong situations with the wrong people, where outbursts of anger quickly turned into fights.

I told her that after I became a Christian I never got into another fight because I avoided putting myself in situations with people who were angry. The moral for her was to pick her friends wisely and it proved to be a real turning point. Mindy has two beautiful children, a girl and a boy. She is a wonderful person and mother and I have dreams for both of her children, as well as for Sam's kids, to become all that God has called them to be.

My other daughter, Sam, suffered with the loss of her mother simply because she felt closer to her and her family than to me. Sam felt she was the favorite of her mother and her mother's family. She also looks like her mother and mother's family. So she felt responsible for her mom and her role changed from daughter to mother. She felt that she could take care of her mother when she couldn't take care of herself yet.

That love and commitment made it hard for her to jump into another family structure with Mindy and me. During Sam's junior high years, I received a lot of messages from her teachers asking me to meet with them. They all said she was a great girl and that they really liked her, but she wouldn't do anything they asked her to do. She had an extreme problem with authority.

But she matured and that problem slowly went away over time. Interestingly, Sam now has three young sons. She's as good a mother as I have ever seen and she demands from her boys that they submit to authority. I guess those early lessons took hold. She saw the difference in the way in which people operate in God's kingdom and the way they live in the kingdom of this world.

My daughters' lessons aren't just kid stories. The way that the girls adapted to a new family structure and their acceptance of authority are the same adjustments inmates have to make as they leave prison or jail. That lack of respect for authority also is likely to be one reason why many men and women make it to prison – they will not be told what to do.

It's an ego thing, too, and a law of the jungle, that if you give in to someone else, they immediately have power or superiority over you – they're ahead of you in society's pecking order. But Jesus asks us to forget all that. He tells us that we need to focus more on the long-term goal of Heaven and how to live the life that Christ has called us to live. I feel better about bowing to authority when I remember that I surrendered my life to Jesus more than two decades ago.

The Apostle Paul often wrote of authority in his many letters. Paul writes about why it's so important to obey Earthly authority.

Romans 13

1 Everyone must submit himself to the governing authorities, for there is no authority except that which God has established. The authorities that exist have been established by God.

2 Consequently, he who rebels against the authority is rebelling against what God

has instituted, and those who do so will bring judgment on themselves.

3 For rulers hold no terror for those who do right, but for those who do wrong. Do you want to be free from fear of the one in authority? Then do what is right and he will commend you.

4 For he is God's servant to do you good. But if you do wrong, be afraid, for he does not bear the sword for nothing. He is God's servant, an agent of wrath to bring punishment on the wrongdoer.

5 Therefore, it is necessary to submit to the authorities, not only because of possible punishment but also because of conscience.

That explains why breaking the law is such a devastating sin. Those of us who've committed those criminal acts might have paid our debts to society with our prison sentences, but the question remains of whether we've changed inside. Earlier in Romans, Paul shows that respecting authority is even more important for our souls since we all have only so long to bow to Earthly authorities and that our rewards for that obedience will be great. It's a very important way in which to show others that we have changed. So, if you belong to Christ, be consistent with who you were.

Romans 7

1 Do you not know, brothers – for I am speaking to men who know the law – that the law has authority over a man only as long as he lives?

4 So, my brothers, you also died to the law through the body of Christ, that you might belong to another, to him who was raised from the dead, in order that we might bear fruit to God.

5 For when we were controlled by the sinful nature, the sinful passions aroused by the law were at work in our bodies, so that we bore fruit for death.

6 But now, by dying to what once bound us, we have been released from the law so that we serve in the new way of the Spirit, and not in the old way of the written code.

Chapter Twelve

The Scope of God's Plan

Before the break-up of the Soviet Union, trips behind the Iron Curtain were hardly simple. Visitors were advised to have their traveling papers – meaning passport and visa – in order. The Russian military wasn't known to be kind or friendly – and the Welcome Wagon hadn't established any Russian chapters at that time, at least as far as I knew. It was not a stretch to say that foreigners traveling to Moscow alone could be easy targets for thieves – inside the ruling army and out.

But the question is, with all of the security, all of the paranoia toward Americans, how does an ex-prisoner from Iowa get inside the heart of Russia and speak to men and women in prisons there? How does that happen?

God only knows. He led me there in 1991.

I endured hours alone in the Moscow airport, sat through an enlightening session with the KGB, feared for my life during a nighttime ride with those notorious agents on a desolate Russian highway, and lived to tell about it. It all had to be part of God's plan.

The trip was arranged by a Canadian Christian businessman. I met this man when I was asked to speak at the 1990 annual convention of the National Baptist Church held in Oklahoma City. After hearing me speak about my work in prison ministry, a man came up to me and introduced himself as a Christian businessman from Ottawa, Canada. He asked me if I thought I'd ever like to go to the Soviet Union to preach the Gospel in the prisons there. My response was, "You know, Chuck Colson and others have just returned from there. Wouldn't you rather have one of them come?" He looked at me and said, "No, I want you." I said I'd love to. He said he would arrange it and I gave him my business card and forgot all about it. I thought he was just blowing smoke, but he called my office in Kansas City one day a few months later and said he had it all arranged. "When would you like to go?" he asked. "What do I need to do?" I asked him. "Raise about $8,000," he said, "and I'll take care of the rest."

He told me he would arrange for my visa in

Canada and have it sent to my office. The visa never came. Somehow or other, it got lost. So the day that I was supposed to catch a plane in Kansas City bound for New York, then to Moscow, I didn't have a visa. My friends in Kansas City said, "Well, you can't go. There's no reason to go. If you don't have a visa, you can't get into the country."

But I knew I had to go. "You know, they've got all of these meetings set up," I told my friends. "I just feel like I have to give it a shot. I'll give it a try. I might not ever get there, but I'll try"

I flew to New York City and I got to the ticket counter to switch planes for the flight to Moscow. The lady asked for my visa. I told her I didn't have it. "You can't go to Moscow without a visa, sir," she said.

I'm such a fast talker; I can talk most people into anything. "I have meetings set up in Russia," I told her. "Call the Russian embassy in Ottawa. They sent me the visa, but it has gotten lost. See what they have to say." She called the Russian embassy in Ottawa. Yes, they told her, there had been a visa issued. Yes, it must be lost. Put him on the plane and we'll make sure there's a visa waiting for him when he arrives at the airport in Moscow. They let me board.

When we arrived in Moscow at 10 p.m., at the checkpoint, I was expecting that not only were the

Christian people who'd arranged the trip going to be there to pick me up, a visa was going to be there, too.

Unlike any airports here, Russian airports were run by the military at that time. There were soldiers walking around with machine guns strapped to their shoulders. The guy at customs was in the military, in a full dress uniform. He asked for my papers and I showed him my passport. "Visa," he said. "Visa please."

I began telling him my story about why I didn't have a visa. I got about halfway through and he clicked his fingers, snap, snap. He waved two more soldiers over. They spoke to each other in Russian and pretty soon, one soldier took an arm, the second took the other arm, and they led me to the other end of the airport, to an office. Two men in suits were waiting in the office. Obviously, they were KGB agents. They began to interrogate me. They had my passport, so they knew who I was, where I was from, all that. But they still asked who I was, what was I doing there. "What made you think you could enter the Soviet Union without a visa?" asked the man who appeared to be the lead agent.

It's not that I thought I could, I told him. I just thought I should try because of these many reasons: Meetings were set up in prisons, people were relying on me, people had given me money for my trip, tickets were bought and paid for that were not refundable.

He sat back in his chair. "Do you have any money?" he asked.

Well, having grown up on the streets, I knew that when somebody started talking about money, it was just a matter of negotiation: How much money?

"I've got a little," I told him.

"You got any U.S. dollars?" he asked.

I nodded again. "I've got a little."

"For 75 U.S. dollars, I'll make you a visa right here," he said.

The other man in the office couldn't speak English, or at least he didn't try. As a matter of fact, he didn't say anything. When the lead agent said he'd make me a visa right there for $75, I saw a typewriter on the desk. I looked over at the typewriter and I looked back at him. "You know what?" I told him. "Get that typewriter over there warmed up because you just cut yourself a deal."

I had put $1,200 in my boot for the trip. I took the money out and peeled off $75. I gave it to him, and he made the visa right there.

He called the soldiers into the room again and they took me back to the checkpoint. I gave the soldier in charge my freshly made visa, they ran me through customs, and then I was standing all alone in the middle of the Moscow airport – still nobody there to pick me up. All I had was the name of a Russian man that I couldn't even pronounce. No phone numbers, nothing, just the name. There was very little activity in the airport. I couldn't even find anyone who spoke English. I was standing there with my suitcases, thinking, "What the heck am I going to do now?"

All of a sudden, the KGB agent who made my $75 visa came up to me. "What are you doing still here?" he asked.

"Well, nobody's here to pick me up," I told him. "I can't find anybody."

"Well you can't stay here," he said.

"Man, I know I can't stay here," I said. "I understand that, but I don't know where to go. I don't know what to do."

"Get yourself a cab, go to downtown Moscow and figure out what you're going to do tomorrow, because you've got to get out of here," he said. "This place is full of robbers. You won't last 'til morning here."

I got frustrated. "I understand perfectly what you're talking about," I said, "but if I call a cab, if I do get somebody on the other end who speaks English, where am I going to tell him I want to go when I know nothing about it?"

He said he could understand my point. "Why don't we do this, I'll take you to downtown Moscow," he said, "drop you off at a hotel."

I was excited. I had found another break.

But, maybe I should have prayed a little harder.

It started to feel like a scene from a movie. It was early January and driving rain and sleet were pelting the pavement. It was pitch dark and a little black car whisked up. The front door opened, I slid in. The KGB agent threw my suitcases in the back and the little car whizzed off into the dark.

I looked around and saw I was in the little car with three Russian men – huge Russian men – and the only one who could speak English was the KGB agent in the seat behind me. All of sudden, it dawned on me that this man knew that I had all of that money on me. I was totally convinced that I was facing the end of my life; that they were going to take me somewhere, kill me, and rob me. I was convinced of that. And maybe no one would ever find my body until after the thaw.

We started driving down the highway, going five or six miles. Now, the highways there aren't lighted like they are in the U.S. They're pitch black. The car suddenly pulled over. This must be it, I thought. They were going to take me into the woods by the side of the road and kill me.

I had been praying the whole time. "God, this is probably the stupidest thing I've ever done in my life," I told Him. "But help me somehow."

Back in the car, the only thing I knew to do was to try some intimidation. I heard the back door open. I turned around and got right up in the face of the agent who gave me the $75 visa. "Where do you think you're going, man?"

Surprised, he looked back at me. "Oh, I live near here," he said. "They're dropping me off and taking you on to Moscow. Relax, relax. We're not robbers."Now what do you think when someone tells you he's not a robber? You think all the more that he is a robber. It was like he read my mind. He got out and the little car spun back out onto the dark highway. We drove a few more miles and they were speaking Russian so there was no communication with me. I thought, well, there were only two guys so my odds were a little better. We came into a town with apartments and other buildings and we continued to drive. I thought, OK, they weren't going to kill me in the woods, but they probably were going to take me to someone's apartment and kill me there. But at least I was in a town where there might be other people around; my odds continued to improve.

Then, the car pulled into this really slum-filled area of town. We stopped in front of a small building. I looked out the window and the building looked like it could be a hotel – an old hotel. The huge Russians got out of the car; one guy went in and came out a few minutes later. The other guy took my suitcases out of the trunk. Standing there, one agent pointed to the door.

I peeled off $20 for them. I was so elated! I would have given them all $1,125 I had left after the airport visa deal. I was so happy after realizing that I wasn't living the last minutes of my life! I still didn't know what I was going to do then, but at least I wasn't going to die.

I went inside and I got a room.

They called it a "room" and not an oversized closet, which it was. It was probably twelve feet long by eight feet wide, with a little half-cot and nightstand with a lamp on it. In the corner was a commode; not with a wall around it, but like you have in a prison cell. I was so exhausted. I had been on the plane for a day or more getting to Moscow, I had been through that ordeal, and I was physically and emotionally worn out. So I just dropped my suitcases on the floor and I fell back onto my cot. But my mind wouldn't let me rest because I still knew that I was in the middle of Moscow with a Russian man's name that I couldn't even pronounce. I had $1,005 left. The lady got me for $120 for the tiny room. What else could I do but pay? But at the rate I was going, my money wasn't going to last too long. So what was I going to do?

I was praying, trying to think of what to do. Suddenly, the words "American Embassy" came to me. That was the first time I had ever been to a foreign country. I didn't know about embassies. But I got up and went downstairs. It was about 2 a.m. and I finally got the phone number for the U.S. Embassy and I called. A young marine sergeant answered. His name was Jim. So I told him my story, who I was, what had happened to me. He listened.

"Oh, Mr. Sharp," he said. "I can't believe what you've been through. Why don't you find somebody who can tell me what that name is on the paper and I'll make some phone calls. You can go back to your room, try to get some rest and I'll see if I can't locate somebody."

I did all that. At about 7 a.m. the next morning, the sergeant called. "I've found the people who were supposed to meet you at the airport," he said. "They got there about 45 minutes after you left. They asked around if anyone had traveled in from the West. They were told about one who left the airport with three guys about an hour earlier."

They thought – as I had feared the night before – that robbers probably had taken me out and left me for dead somewhere.

By God's grace I wasn't dead and I was able to meet my contacts from the Moscow church. They came to pick me up and brought me to another hotel where they had a room reserved for me. They had the whole trip arranged, two weeks worth of meetings, everything set up.

We started going to the various prisons and different speaking events that they had scheduled for me.

The trip that began as an unforgettably frightening mix of uncertain air travel and certain danger with the infamous KGB soon became an incredible Christian story.

I often say that we, as Christians, get caught up in the notion that God seems to use Christian cookie-cutters; making a bunch of cookies that look alike, talk alike, and act alike. My trip to the former Soviet Union helped me understand how wrong that notion is. I was speaking in a prison in Volfe, Ukraine, on the border of Poland. Volfe is an old Eastern European city, 700-800 years old. I was scheduled to speak at a big adult prison there. The only person they could find to interpret for me was a city councilman. The councilman and I, and a couple of local deacons of the church in the city, went to the prison together. I spoke there, gave a very simple message of who Christ is and how He has a claim on our lives. Then I asked the important question: "Is there anybody who wants to know this God I've been talking about?"

No sooner than the interpreter had the question out of his mouth, 300 hands shot into the air simultaneously. Each man in the crowd raised a hand.

The councilman-interpreter got so excited. He'd never seen anything like it. On the way out, he couldn't stop talking about it. He was just so incredibly excited about this experience. I told him that I'd love to see the city. Maybe someone could take me around and show me its landmarks, talk about its history.

"I'd love to take you," he said. I told him I had a free afternoon the next day and suggested he pick me up and show me around.

"Oh, they're not going to let you go with me," he said of the people who had arranged my trip. I asked him why. "Well," he said, "you see, they're Baptists and I'm Orthodox. They've been trying to convert me to be a Baptist for five years. They'll be afraid that I will convert you to Orthodox."

I thought, well where have I heard of this kind of thing before? But I told him we should give it a shot; we should ask, see what they say. We got back to my hotel room and two deacons from the church that brought me to the Soviet Union spoke Russian with the councilman. They were on the other side of the room and they were getting louder, their hands were flying. I thought the conversation wasn't going well, that they probably wouldn't let me go. Finally, the councilman came over and said they agreed to allow him to go with me, but they had to send a driver with us. He was supposed to watch us, to have his eye on us all the time.

My councilman-friend came by to pick me up the next day. We spent three hours together as he took me all over the city. It was incredible. I went to cathedrals that were at least six hundred years old. I was amazed. On the way back to my hotel, he told me he would love for me to meet his wife and two sons. I told him I'd love to meet his family and told him to come by my room the next evening and pick me up again. "Oh, they'll never let you come to my house," he said of the Baptist officials. I knew it was probably because of the same reason. "They've been trying to convert me for five years and they've never been to my house," he said. "They won't come to my house."

Again, I suggested we ask. He did and they had another conversation complete with hand gestures and loud talking, in Russian, of course. "They're going to let you come," he said, "and the driver's going to stand outside the door. When he knocks, you've got to go."

We went to his house and he introduced me to

his family. He had taught his wife and sons, ages ten and eight, to speak English. They had a tiny apartment. His wife ran into the kitchen to make some cheese and crackers and we just sat in the living room to talk. Soon, he jumped up and ran over to a cabinet. He opened one of the doors and pulled out a bottle of liquor. He put it on the table and told me it was a bottle of cognac that had been in his family for 70 years. "As a family, we have been waiting for an honorable time to open it. You being in my home as a representative of Jesus Christ is the most honorable thing that could ever happen to my family. He opened that bottle and he, his wife, and I had a little drink of cognac in honor of Christ. I had tears in my eyes.

Then came the knock at the door. My host jumped up, ran off, and then came back with a handful of candy. "Here, eat this," he said. "If those Baptists smell alcohol on your breath, they'll have my head on a platter."

On the way home, I looked over at him and he had tears in his eyes. I put my hand on his shoulder and asked him if he was OK "I am just overwhelmed that you would come to my home," he said. "You must be like Jesus."

I knew the truth. "Buddy," I said, "I am probably very little like Jesus, but let me tell you something: If Jesus were here, He would be honored to come to your home and be with your family.

It was such an electrifying, powerful moment. Ironically, the people trying to convert him for five years wouldn't even come to his house. Jesus would have gone to his house. In fact, in his lifetime, Jesus was rebuked for doing such things. Paraphrasing the book of Matthew in the Bible, "John's disciples fasted, they didn't eat with sinners, they didn't drink with sinners. Here you are eating and drinking with sinners." One of Jesus' responses to that situation was to say, "Hey, it isn't the healthy that need a doctor, it's the sick."

Just like my whole trip to the former Soviet Union in 1991, it's evidence of God's plan.

Chapter Thirteen

From Weakness, Strength

My life in prison ministry hasn't been one adventurous trip after another. I was blessed by God to go to the former Soviet Union and meet the people there. I was also blessed, in a way, to survive the trip, but you already know that story.

As great as the rewards are for me – and there's no other job on Earth that I'd rather have – reaching inmates' hearts can be hard work. One of the problems we face in helping prisoners now is that every cult known to man wants to bring its message inside prison walls every week. They all want to share their particular read on what salvation is and how they can help inmates reach it.

Can you imagine how confusing that is for the prisoners? Even those becoming secure in their Christian faith might hear somebody different every week who spouts a different doctrine, a different take on the situation. They hear that if they don't speak in tongues, they're not saved or if they're not baptized a certain way, they're not saved. The procession of different Christian approaches alone can shake their faith.

Then there's even greater competition – and confusion – from cults, Muslims, and white witchcraft. Yes, even witchcraft is a viable religion in prison now. It's total confusion! So, in most cases, inmates don't really have anybody who can just spend time with them and guide them through those feelings they have when they become new believers.

My Soviet Union trip made a lasting impression on inmates in the Ukraine – and on prisoners at the well-known Leavenworth prison in Kansas. The impact didn't come from anything I said so much as from what I brought.

I worked for Prison Fellowship as the state director for Kansas when I went on that 1991 trip. I had a pretty good relationship with a group of about thirty inmates at the U.S. Penitentiary in Leavenworth, where those inmates had become a church of their own. About a month before I left for Russia, I told them about my trip, how excited I was to be going, and about preaching the Gospel to prisoners in Russia. The Leavenworth inmates got a card and signed it. They gave me the card and asked me to give it to the inmates in a prison in Russia as a gift from them and to tell them that their American brothers were praying for them.

So, in a men's maximum-security prison in the Ukraine, I gave the card to a group of men who already had confessed their faith in Christ. "This card is from a group of prisoners who are now your brothers," I told the men in the Ukraine. A couple of them quickly left the room. When they returned, they had a card. Every member of the group signed it and gave it to me to bring back to the men in Leavenworth. I told the Leavenworth inmates that these men that they had never met, likely never would meet this side of Heaven, were now their brothers and that they were praying for them as well.

The Leavenworth inmates were very excited and grateful to get the return card. They felt like they shared a bond with the Ukrainians. Both groups of prisoners knew that they wouldn't get out of prison for years – some might never get out – but now they had proof, a tangible piece of evidence that they were part of something so much larger than their five-by-nine prison cells.

The Leavenworth prisoners felt an immediate kinship with the men in the Ukraine. Together, they became an example of Christ's teaching: "We are one body." These guys felt they were part of something they won't see until eternity.

We have a captive audience when we go into prisons, but we face a completely different set of issues when the inmates we've been counseling and evangelizing start to make parole.

Statistics have shown that there's a very short span of time after release from prison that will tell whether a man or woman is going to continue on in their faith. Say they've been walking with Christ effectively for five years in prison. When they're released, there's just a small window, seventy-two hours, that will tell whether that former inmate will continue to walk with Christ or go back to the world.

The difference comes down to whether they have somebody there as a friend, as a Christian, from the moment they're released. So, if an inmate gets out of prison, hops a bus back to Des Moines, Iowa, somebody should be there at the bus station. They can go have a cup of coffee and that simple act tells the inmate that somebody is there for them. They're connected. That's the start to helping them stay away from their old friends and family. It's very important.

You go from the inability to satisfy any temptation in jail to opportunities for immediate satisfaction on the outside. It's a powerful change in circumstances. It also comes at a very vulnerable time. A wheelbarrow of emotions starts flooding into your life. You've been sitting in a prison cell for five years, dreaming about the day you get out, the day you go back to your husband or wife, boyfriend, girlfriend or family, or just get out in general. That flood of emotions hits you and renders you very vulnerable at that moment.

When we go into prisons we bring prisoners the message of Jesus' saving work. Of course, this oportunity gives us, as ex-prisoners, immediate access to their hearts. We have credibility, which gives us that immediate access. If you go to a prison, or any other setting for that matter, and you have that kind of credibility and openness, the people are not on the defensive.

The group of prisoners that most people might expect to be impossible to reach would be the "Lifers," men and women who know they'll probably never leave prison. Often model prisoners, Lifers understand that prison is all they have, all they're ever going to have. So they make the best of it. They make it work because their existence behind forty-foot walls and razor wire is all they're ever going to know.

At the same time, a lifer's heart is open and sometimes fertile enough for them to understand their sin and be intimately acquainted with it and seek the forgiveness that Christ has to offer. It all goes back to the heart again. Without the heart being open to Christ by the work of the Holy Spirit, the seed just falls on rocky ground. It's there for a moment and it's gone. It's important for the heart to be receptive. That's why ex-prisoners are so effective in prison outreach efforts; hearts are immediately opened to men and women coming in to tell their stories. Nearly all inmates have core experiences in their lives before, during, and after their sentences. They feel and know that the stories they hear from former inmates could just as easily be their own stories. They know that we've been there, so they are far more receptive.

One of the biggest obstacles we face in working with inmates is dealing with their hardships of being disconnected from their families. They feel like they'll never be completely connected with their families when they get out. I became acquainted with a lifer throughout the first six months of 2001. He experienced some heartbreak in June that easily could have been avoided if he'd communicated his feelings a little differently. His example might help a lot of other prisoners.

The day after Father's Day, I asked the inmate if his two children had visited with him over the weekend. (I'm not using his name because I don't want to violate his privacy or his family's.) "They didn't," he said sadly. "I don't know how it's going work out."

He was talking about trying to make the family relationship work out, about staying involved in the lives of his children, if not the life of their mother, too, who is now his ex-wife. He knew she was doing a great job of raising the kids after he'd gone to jail, helping them cope with the burden of being the children of a convict. Because of all the work she was doing for the children, he was beginning to believe that the kids would be better off if he stayed out of the picture. Not having a Father's Day visit from the kids began to confirm his feelings.

But I talked to the prisoner's ex-wife. She said she didn't bring the kids for a visit because she'd heard from the prisoner's mother that he'd told her that the ex-wife was doing such a good job that he didn't feel worthy of a visit from the kids. So, through poor communication and his own feelings of low esteem, he denied himself a visit from his children.

Even though he is a believer, the prisoner feels unworthy because of the deep-rooted agony that he's destroyed his family's life. Most inmates like this man aren't worried about whether God forgives them. That's their strength and they grasp that. But the difficult part is for them to learn to forgive themselves. Like many prisoners, they put themselves in bondage to shame and unworthiness.

That's a weakness.

But God can change things. That's what we try to explain to inmates. If we repent and turn to Christ, God may give us the opportunity to see our families sometime down the road.

In some ways, I was like that prisoner when I was in jail. I struggled with the same problems of sin and shame – but I didn't know Christ. My heart wasn't receptive.

And now God has given me the truth that I need about myself to communicate effectively. It's now so great to be doing God's work, serving Him first and making a big difference in the lives of men and women in prison. I didn't have to end up where I am now. I could have gone the way of others doing the same things I was doing: robbing, taking drugs, living close to the edge in a reckless, misguided life. But God took something close to worthless in an Earthly sense and made it worthwhile. He transformed me. I also don't know if I, or anyone, would choose the course I've taken to get to this point. But we all have to remember that God says He works all things out for good for those called to His purposes.

There's a passage in the New Testament, Hebrews 11, verses 33-34, that might help explain how my earlier life of sin now helps me serve God.

Hebrews 11

33 who through faith conquered kingdoms, administered justice, and gained what was promised; who shut the mouths of lions,

34 quenched the fury of the flames, and escaped the edge of the sword; whose weakness was turned to strength; and who became powerful in battle and routed foreign armies.

All of the things that happened to me – the things I was a part of and had to endure – all of those weaknesses have become my greatest strengths. Maybe I didn't have to go through what I did, but through God's grace, I got here and He's making the most of my life now.

Chapter Fourteen

The Message and the Meaning

The message.

That's it. That's the single most important piece of any ministry. For it is the foundation for all that we should say and do. Whether for us at Prison Impact or anyone else, the message has to come first. The simple message of Christianity tells of God's love, hope, and forgiveness of sin through Jesus' death on the cross and His resurrection.

The message, of course, is eternal salvation.

But many times it isn't easy for everyone to understand. I had heard about God having a plan for my life, but it didn't make much sense to me. It's like the well-known saying, "You can't see the forest for the trees." I couldn't see how God cared for me, had a plan for me, because I was running around doing everything God tries to teach us not to do – all of the things that bring so much pain and loss to our lives. But when God broke through, I finally figured things out.

Once I recognized God's love and presence in my life, I found it easier to share the message that I know is true: Christ died for sinners like me. I tell a lot of stories when I visit prisons all over the country and even if I didn't know about the message, I still could tell the stories of my past and inmates would see how my life parallels their own. But since I now know the message, I can tell them how my experiences and theirs fit in God's love and in His plan. God says that He takes the weakest of us to show forth His miracles and strength. I am who I am today because of the road that I have traveled. It shows an unbelieving world that God is alive and still involved in the lives of those He has chosen.

I like to tell one story from my old life in the burglary ring during the 1960s that explains how we run and hide from God's judgment.

In one of our less successful jobs, we found out that a local supermarket kept a lot of money in its safe on a certain day of the month. That was all the motivation we needed: There was cash in the building, a lot of it. All we had to do was get in there and take it.

So, one hot summer night, after midnight, we drove to the market to break in, crack the safe and take the money. We carried guns that night. I still don't know why, but it wasn't a habit. We could never be sure of what might happen. Not the smartest thing to do, but we had them nevertheless. Nick and Joe climbed up on the store's roof as I stood in the alley behind the store to watch for anything out of the ordinary.

We thought we had everything covered that night. Nick and Joe were on top of the building, trying to rip a hole in it, while I stood in a perfect position to see anyone coming from any direction. We had walkie-talkies and we were talking about the job. Then, the lights hit.

They flashed on from so many directions. All of a sudden, the blinding lights told me the whole area was filled with police. They didn't let us know they were coming until they were all over the place. Someone must have seen or heard us because they were prepared.

I called Nick and Joe on the walkie-talkies. I yelled to them that the police were all around the building; that they were on their way up to the roof. I told them to get out of there. We split in different directions. I raced into the park next to the market. It had the kind of cover I needed and if it hadn't been there, I couldn't have gotten away.

On the way into the woods of the park, I shot a couple of rounds at the cops chasing me. All that I had on my mind was to somehow get out of there. My heart was pounding from sheer adrenalin. I moved through the park as fast as I could, dodging trees and imagined danger. I don't think I slowed down at all as I pointed the gun back at the police again and shot another round. As they shot back, I ran all the faster. The escape didn't seem to be headed for success as I kept shooting and hiding behind trees in the park.

It was dark and I had no way of knowing which way to go, where the trouble was, or if I'd get out alive. I was still clinging to the notion that my criminal life on Earth was worth killing someone else. I hadn't yet heard that the life after this one was the one that counted most. I was still Godless, directionless. So, there I was, bouncing around the woods. My only concern was to avoid getting caught – or shot.

I dashed from tree to tree, running the short distances in full sprints. I never saw exactly how many police showed up at the market, but I knew that they had three or four squad cars. That meant that there could have been as many as a dozen cops chasing us as we ran. I heard one of the policemen yell, "Halt!" I got behind one tree and turned to look back to see where they were. Immediately, the bark exploded from the tree that shielded me. Inches in his aim and splinters of bark were all that kept me out of a coffin – and helped me avoid a meeting that I just wasn't ready for.

Even though I was out of breath from the chase through the wooded park, I found a last burst of energy and made it to the edge of the woods. Ahead of me was a bridge that would lead me across the Des Moines River. I just had to make it across that bridge before the police saw me, but that would put me out in the open, totally exposed. I had to find a way to avoid being seen.

I didn't take the bridge. I chose to swim across the river from the east side, where the supermarket and the park were, to the west side, where I lived. By that time, it was two or three in the morning. I swam, stopping in shallow areas to rest. I remember that it wasn't very deep and it took me about twenty minutes to make it across. I think that the police had given up on catching me by the time I got in the water, but my paranoid mind figured they were right behind me and closing in.

But they weren't. Maybe the police chasing me turned back to help the others who were trying to track down Nick and Joe. They made it down safely from the roof. Nick ran into the park, too, running all around another part of the woods. He lived nearby and made it all the way home that night – where he had a solid, if not truthful, alibi if the police had found him there.

Joe got away, too. He got a couple of blocks away from the market we were trying to rob. He ran down the street looking for someplace to hide, someplace to escape. He found a parked car that was unlocked and got in and laid down on the floor. He stayed there all night.

What I try to show inmates now is that my racing through the park, darting from tree to tree, shooting at the police as they shot at me, is the way they go through life. "With no direction, nothing to guide you," I say to them. "It's so easy to get into trouble. Or, more accurately, trouble will find you."

We all seem to run and hide. The Bible says we've been doing it ever since Adam and Eve tried to hide from God, ducking behind the tree in the Garden as He came to fellowship with them. I thought I was running from the police, but I was running from the path God had already chosen for me that I knew nothing about.

It doesn't have to be that way for you, though. Just like I managed to end my running and escape that period of my life – by a few inches and a couple of splinters of bark – you can, too. Now I have a light whose name is Jesus that takes me from one place to another. You – anyone – can have the same guide to lead you.

Obviously, not everyone is willing to accept

this message. Many choose to continue in the cycle of violence and lawlessness – including drugs and other addictions. I found a way out. Many others have found the same simple way out as well.

Around 1996, twenty years after I left Anamosa, the staff there asked me to come back to be a part of a twenty-year anniversary event: It was billed as "Still Free 20 Years After Prison." I went and what I found there was a mix of feelings. I thought that I was prepared for it, but all the preparation didn't make me feel any better about what I came face to face with.

I saw men there who were in prison on their third or fourth sentence, doing "life" on the installment plan. Many of them had been there when I was at Anamosa two decades before. They had been paroled, gone back, been paroled again and were now back. They couldn't seem to make the right choices in order to stay free.

It's natural to feel joy when you see an old friend that you haven't seen for many years. I had those feelings of delight upon seeing many of the men I knew all those years before. But more than any other feeling, I felt sadness at the tragedy. I could see the pain in their faces, the sense of loss that they felt. Faces held the wrinkles of time, the marks of hard living, of not taking care of themselves. Their stares were gray and empty, showing the burdens they carried in the prison they had created for themselves.

Murderers, robbers, pushers, and drug addicts. They all looked up at me as if to say, "Take us out of here, put us on the track you've found."

I can tell them I've done the crimes that most of them have committed. I can tell them that I used to lie awake in my cell at nights feeling that I had absolutely no hope of ever finding anything better. That I used to lie in my cell at night feeling all of the feelings that they do.

That's when I get emotional bringing the message to inmates. I tell them I know how it feels to stand in line for hours at the prison post office, hoping for a letter that never comes. I've gotten up Saturday mornings, cleaned myself up, shaved, and gotten prepared for a visit that never happened. I tell them I've felt every feeling that they've ever felt. And so has Christ, the second person of the Trinity, in His human nature. For Hebrews 4:15 says, "For we do not have a high priest who is unable to sympathize with our weaknesses, but we have one who has been tempted in every way, just as we are - yet was without sin."

When I begin to talk about that, there's something that engages them and my stories are no longer just stories at that point. I've dug into the emotions I felt while I was in prison, the same emotions they're feeling right then. There's anger, intense anger that wells up to the surface. I felt anger when I was an inmate, but it was because my life before Christ was centered in my sinful behavior. Still, the years that have passed since I've been out of prison don't matter as I stand and speak to them about their sinful behavior and the hope the believer has in the gospel. I feel the same emotions and desires that they do. At those times, I see the results of their sin and I'm transported back to the time when I was a prisoner. I guess it's what God does to keep me humble enough to be effective.

But, I can't help them unless God reveals the truth of the gospel to them.

The true message of the gospel (literally "good news") is a message about a past historical event. The gospel is about the completed work of Christ on behalf of His people. 1 Corinthians 15:2-4 says,

> *By this gospel you are saved, if you hold firmly to the word I preached to you. Otherwise, you have believed in vain. For what I received I passed on to you as of first importance: that Christ died for our sins according to the Scriptures, that he was buried, that he was raised on the third day according to the Scriptures,*

Christ calls us to repent and believe the gospel. But what is true repentance? It is not being sorry for being caught and now being in prison. Repentance does include being sorry for sins, but it is much more. A person who truly repents is a person who recognizes sin for what it ultimately is, an offense against a Holy God.

Repentance is a life long disposition of turning away from sin and toward Christ. In other words, it is not your righteousness that saves you but His righteousness. True repentance does not turn from sin to self effort, but rests in the completed work of Christ for their salvation.

John 4:17
From that time on Jesus began to preach, "Repent, for the kingdom of heaven is near."

Chapter Fifteen

Facing Problems

One of many things that bothered me while I was a prisoner was that I was told that I had antisocial behavior. It was more than an identification. Because of that label, I was lumped into a greater group of men and women who were considered social outcasts. From a psychologist's perspective, I wasn't able to associate and assimilate into society. I used to get so mad at the label that the hair on the back of my neck stood up. I resisted it, denied it, and became upset whenever anyone talked about it. Yes, I'm sure that I did exhibit antisocial behavior. At the very least, I saw that for whatever reason I couldn't make it in a free world.

After I became a Christian, I faced the reality that what they were saying was true. There was much about Ron Sharp that was antisocial.

If I was ever going to become a part of this greater group, the working group that God calls a church, I was going to have to learn how to be part of something bigger than myself. I was going to have to put myself in positions that were extremely uncomfortable for me, such as going to church and, after getting there, becoming a part of it. I put myself at risk just by going to church because it was uncomfortable – not to mention the fact that it made people aware of parts of my life that left me extremely vulnerable, namely that I had been in prison

Here we are, twenty-four years later, and I still face a tug of war inside at times. I could very easily isolate myself at home for a year – never seeing another human being – and it wouldn't bother me much. But there is another part of me that knows and believes, senses and wants to be a living, breathing example for others – once again putting myself in places where I am very uncomfortable.

I cope with this problem by remembering Jesus' teachings. He said He trusted no man for He knew what was in the hearts of men. Yet he did put himself in positions of vulnerability in His relationships with human beings and He expects it of me as well.

I can live with being uncomfortable because I know that my story is more than the average story of an ex-prisoner – I have found the way to really be free and my story is one that needs to be told.

But building ministries takes more than a story. It takes more than prayer and sheer hard work, too – though plenty of both are required. Ministries need cash and, no matter what our calling is, we all have to do our parts to raise money. I help raise money for Prison Impact by speaking to church organizations, pastoral groups, and other people in hopes of getting financial assistance and to help spread the word of what God is doing in the lives of prisoners.

I enjoy the process because I believe in what we do and I know that it's God that changes the lives of prisoners. All we need to remember is that we work for Him. It's up to me to communicate to people the amazing nature of what we do and to show the credibility that I have – that I'm not just out to take their money. In the end, God brings the resources.

But it's still fun to remind people of the humble – and criminal – nature of my past. I often open fund-raising speeches with a little dark humor: "You know, I used to rob people with a sawed-off shotgun," I tell them. "Now, I just talk 'em out of their money! Which would you rather I do today?"

That opening is sometimes met with laughter

and sometimes with silence. A former prisoner and criminal talking to pastors and others about money seems to be at least a little odd.

But I'm convinced that what we're doing becomes more necessary every day. Criminologists and law-abiding members of society continue to push prisons and inmates farther out of the mainstream. For years, the trend has been building to punish criminals with stiffer, longer sentences. But that's not the answer.

Some say that rehabilitation should come before punishment if we really want to change the behavior. Unfortunately, changing inmates seems to be merely a thought that has long since passed. As much as rehabilitation might help inmates change their outward behavior, it's the change that God makes inwardly that gives them the strength to live out their lives in obedience to both God and man. God makes the inward changes and those changes are easily seen in inmates' outward behavior.

Any beliefs I held inside me always showed up on the outside – before God changed me and after. Until I changed, though, I didn't think much about the consequences of my actions. Or, I was just like most criminals, thinking about the score and never expecting to be caught.

Sometime in my late 'teens, I hooked up with a couple of friends for a really harebrained scheme to rob a bank. We left Des Moines that night and traveled into the farmland that makes up most of Iowa. We planned to drive to their home, kidnap the bank president's family, and hold them for ransom. One of us would stand guard over the family while the other two took the president down to the bank where he would get us into the vault and give us the payroll cash.

It wasn't a very detailed plan. I've forgotten the name of the town and even what part of the state it's in. I had never tried anything so daring before. The rush was overwhelming and the opportunity outweighed the feeling of "what if?" As always, we never thought about getting caught.

What most people don't realize is that criminals don't think about the downside of the crime before they do it. Getting caught? It's just not a part of the planning process. So the impact of getting caught is never thrown in as a negative outcome of the deal.

We didn't think about what might happen if the police happened to show up at the house or the bank. We never considered what might happen if the bank president tried to stop us or if he refused to let us into the vault. We didn't think about the likelihood of anyone getting shot or how much jail time we would get if we were caught. Nothing. We just thought it was an easy scheme to score a lot of cash.

Criminals have the same mindset as athletes – we all start the activity believing we're going to win. Athletes don't think about how they'll feel if they don't come out on top. It's the same mindset for criminals: What am I going to do with the loot I get from this job? The approach isn't realistic, but it's the way the mind works.

When we got to the town, though, we had to deal with something else we hadn't planned for: The family wasn't home. No kidnapping, no ransom, no payroll cash. We hung around for a while and came back to Des Moines.

Whenever I tell that story, I usually add that I'm so fortunate that it didn't work out the way we planned. Otherwise, I might still be in prison somewhere, wondering when or if I'd get out. Taking hostages at gunpoint can get you a life sentence in some states.

So political parties and candidates can promise more jail time, but they won't be right when they say that longer sentences alone will reduce crime. They're usually right when they talk about the number of prisoners leaving jail and then returning in just a few years, though. But they don't discuss the fact that crime and stiffer sentences bring more prisoners into the system, so the percentages don't change.

So if you commit a crime and go to prison, the statistics tell us that two-thirds of all prisoners will be re-arrested within three years of release – according to the U.S. Department of Justice. What this says is that out of one hundred, nearly seventy will either die or grow old as they continue to return to prison. Not really good results.

It's a tragic failure for prisoners, our system, and the entire country. But crimes aren't committed because the punishment isn't tough enough, or because inmates aren't getting the message. Locking people up longer is a convenient way to say you're fixing the problem – but it's not the right way.

That's troubling from a Christian perspective. I don't believe that Jesus would turn his back on prisoners simply because they had strayed from the path he had chosen. His words in the Book of Luke prove that. Jesus responded to Pharisees and teachers of the law who criticized Him for associating with sinners and for welcoming them to join Him in His commitment to God.

Luke 15
3 Then Jesus told them this parable:
4 "Suppose one of you has a hundred sheep and loses one of them. Does he not leave the ninety-nine in the open country and go after

the lost sheep until he finds it?

5 And when he finds it, he joyfully puts it on his shoulders

6 and goes home. Then he calls his friends and neighbors together and says, 'Rejoice with me; I have found my lost sheep.'

7 I tell you that in the same way there will be more rejoicing in heaven over one sinner who repents than over ninety-nine righteous persons who do not need to repent.

But the crucial part is true repentance. Change. You have to give up all the wicked, evil ways you might have had before. No more sin, no more giving in to weakness, thinking that it will be just "one last time." Let the last time be the one you had before you knew what was at stake.

We should all know that as long as we're breathing, it's not too late. One of the most meaningful moments in the Bible comes from the Crucifixion itself. As Jesus nears his last minutes on Earth, He endures taunts from Roman soldiers and the crowd around Him who challenge Him to save Himself if He really is God's Son. The Bible says that the two men crucified with Him were involved in the verbal abuse thrown at Jesus. What made one man change his disposition about Him and not the other? I believe that the one who changed saw what Peter saw from afar that night, and wrote about years later. The abuse was being hurled at Jesus and He was dying, but He said nothing. He trusted His life to His Father in Heaven. The man next to Him came to see – and believe – that he was nailed on a cross next to a dying God. The other man continued in his denial of God and died without Him.

Luke 23

39 One of the criminals who hung there hurled insults at him: "Aren't you the Christ? Save yourself and us!"

40 But the other criminal rebuked him. "Don't you fear God," he said, "since you are under the same sentence?

41 We are punished justly, for we are getting what our deeds deserve. But this man has done nothing wrong."

42 Then he said, "Jesus, remember me when you come into your kingdom."

43 Jesus answered him, "I tell you the truth, today you will be with me in paradise."

Chapter Sixteen

An Uncertain Ending - A Certain Beginning

As the months began to flip off the calendar in 2001, this book moved from a pipe dream – the stage it had occupied for years until the spring – to reality late in the summer. While that was happening, I began to witness an interesting development – literally, a development. From my kitchen window, I now see the tall shingle-sided outside walls of a brand new home beyond my backyard. The new construction sits directly in my view of the house that police surrounded in 1973, to arrest me for the last crime I committed.

It was inevitable, really. No land worthy of developing sits vacant for long. In the same way, the world is developing men to fit into the enemy's plan. Oh yeah, the enemy is Satan, and he has a diabolical plan to get you caught up in his system that will lead you to his kingdom. But at the same time, God is developing men and women to fit into His plan and His kingdom.

Now, there's usually nothing wrong with developing land from an Earthly perspective. From a spiritual point of view, I thought I might be losing something important, a source of inspiration, as the new home blocked more of my view each day. But now, I can see it as a reminder of how God looks at sin. He forgives our sins and covers the wounds they have created.

So the new home built between my window and the house in which I was arrested represents the way God covers the wounds cut in my heart in my younger days – and gives me another unique perspective on life and faith.

But even if I still had a clear view of the old house these days, I would talk to God more about the future and less about the past that I see through the window.

Sometimes, it's hard for me to think about the future. Here I am, in the midst of some of the greatest days and events in my ministry: this book, more chances to bring the Gospel and God's love to inmates, a deeper understanding of God's ways. All of those efforts offer satisfying and powerful evidence of faith and its bounty. I hope they continue for years to come.

I have ongoing heart problems, which at

times drain my energy – a circumstance brought on by that bout of rheumatic fever I had after my father died. But I don't despair. I've faced more frightening, and, it seems, more immediate, danger. I remember so many trials and troubles, like the shootout with the Des Moines Police in the park after they busted up our supermarket burglary. Or the time I laid under the factory's floorboard as rats crawled all around and over me while I waited for the police to leave the area. I was certain I would be robbed and killed in the former Soviet Union, when the KGB agents were driving me into town.

But God had a plan for me. That plan meant that it wasn't my time to go in any of those situations, or at any other point in my past.

I still face a lot of unknown factors in my life now – just as we all do – like I did when I was in and out of prison and local jails. Unlike before, though, I know that there is a God. I know that He holds it all together. Thanks to Him, every day is totally planned for me.

But even now, I still say I gotta get outta here, in anxious anticipation of meeting my Savior. Whether tomorrow is my time, or if it's next week, next month, or next year, I know that I should prepare every day for the most important meeting I'll ever have. I look at this time of my life as my "window" of opportunity. I know that I want to look through this window with nothing but joy.

No matter how good a view I have, I can still sit for hours and look out my kitchen window and think about my life and the many blessings I have: my daughters, my grandchildren, brothers and sisters, and many friends. My life is indeed rich, far richer than I hoped it would be when I was running around as a thief and drug addict. Thanks be to God.

I would love to hear from you and hear about how God has used my story to bring change to your life.

Write to me at:
Ron Sharp
Prison Impact Ministries
P.O.Box 440
Des Moines, Iowa 50302
and http://www.prisonimpact.org

Prison Impact Ministries is a 501 (C) 3 non-profit organization governed by a board of directors.

This edition in the 70 x 7 series, *Reflections Through the Window*, is provided as a free gift to reach juveniles, men and women in correctional facilities throughout the United States.

The continued success of this gift edition depends on personal contributions. Each $3 contribution puts one book in the hands of an inmate and allows Prison Impact to send me or another evangelist to speak to men and women at a prison.

About the Authors

Ron Sharp is now primarily involved with Prison Impact Ministries, headquartered in Kalispell, Montana. He lives in Des Moines, Iowa – in the same neighborhood in which he grew up. Over the course of nearly three decades, he has served as a prison chaplain and a key administrator for the well-known Prison Fellowship Ministries. How he broke out of the cycle of drugs, crime, and prison to reach this point is truly a miracle of God's grace. Growing up in the inner city of Des Moines, Ron got involved with drugs and crime at the young age of thirteen. For the next dozen years, he was destined for prison as drugs controlled his life. They were the catalyst that turned him into a hardened criminal. He spent those years in and out of local jails in Iowa, somehow avoiding prison until 1973, when he was given twenty-five years and sent to Anamosa State Penitentiary. The miracle came in 1977, after Ron had been paroled from Anamosa. After release, he was invited to a church meeting and answered an altar call. His life has not been the same since. Ron continues to visit institutions and help men and women all over the country come to the knowledge that things can be different for them as well.

Michael Clark has written for and edited newspapers and magazines for nearly two decades. He also is the author of the nonfiction book *Reason to Believe*.